Change Your Life Now

Change Your Life Now

Powerful Techniques for Positive Change

Dr. William J. Knaus

Foreword by Albert Ellis, Ph.D.

John Wiley & Sons, Inc.
New York • Chichester • Brisbane • Toronto • Singapore

Library of Congress Cataloging-in-Publication Data

Knaus, William J.
   Change your life now : powerful techniques for positive
change / William J. Knaus.
      p. cm.
   Includes bibliographical references and index.
   ISBN 0-471-00455-3 (pbk.)
   1. Change (Psychology)   2. Self-actualization (Psychology)
I. Title.
BF637.C4K52   1994
155.2'4—dc20   93-36970

Printed in the United States of America

10 9 8 7 6 5 4 3 2 1

I dedicate this book to Albert Ellis in celebration of his eightieth birthday and in recognition of his leadership in the cognitive revolution in psychotherapy, his invention of rational-emotive-behavior therapy, and for his outstanding scholarship and teaching. Without Al's insightful contributions to the field of psychotherapy, this book would never have been written.

I also dedicate this book to my two sons, Billy and Bobby. If for some reason I am not here to watch them grow, I leave them this book of ideas about this marvelous life process we call change.

Acknowledgments

I want to acknowledge the following people who reviewed and gave comments about the earlier drafts of this book: Diana Richman, Ph.D., Stephen Weinrach, Ph.D., Susan Walen, Ph.D., Robert Hard, J.D., and my Thursday morning breakfast club members Joe Costanzo, Ed.D., and Rob Robinson, Ph.D. I particularly want to express my gratitude to Judith McCarthy, my editor at John Wiley & Sons, for her superb effort to make sure that this comprehensive change book was "reader friendly." I especially want to thank my wife Nancy Knaus, M.B.A., Ph.D., for her patience and helpful comments about this book as it evolved through many stages over many years.

Contents

Contents

Foreword

Dr. Bill Knaus has been one of the outstanding practitioners of rational-emotive therapy (RET) for a quarter of a century, is the founder of rational-emotive education (REE), and is a pioneer psychologist in devising rational methods of overcoming procrastination. He has written seven books applying RET and REE to important life problems, and the present one is truly his very best.

Change Your Life Now explores the process of human change, the common ways in which people block their self-changing and self-actualizing activities, and—especially—effective ways to start, to implement, and to continue constructive changing. As usual, Bill's writing style is exceptionally clear, interesting, and highly informative. He is truly a great educator. Almost any reader who is interested in changing himself or herself can distinctly benefit from reading—and unprocrastinatingly using!—this book.

Albert Ellis, Ph.D.
President, Institute for Rational-Emotive Therapy
New York

Part One

Getting Started
Techniques and Strategies for Self-Discovery

1

Beginning the Journey

Are you getting what you want out of life? If you are like most people, you want to love and feel loved. You want to enjoy your leisure time. You want to use your abilities to excel. You want to feel comfortable and self-accepting. You want more job satisfaction and less stress. You want to overcome problem habits such as procrastination, smoking, drinking, or overeating.

Countless people want these same things, but few achieve them. Why? In my thirty years as a psychologist and business consultant, I have discovered one simple reason: Most of us actively resist the idea that change requires positive actions. In a nutshell, changes we want normally won't happen on their own. Once "changers" accept this idea, their desires usually turn out to be within reach.

If you are ready to change your life for the better in order to get what you want now, you have chosen the right book for your guide.

It begins, as all good self-change must, with a journey of self-discovery. Through this journey you can help yourself build confidence in your abilities, see life from more than one angle, strengthen your value system, open yourself to more choices, and maintain a rational perspective. This basic process promotes an inner flexibility to focus on what is important, the power to perform, the resiliency to rebound, and the persistence to prevail. Consider these concepts your foundation for change.

Change Your Life Now gives you a blueprint for change—a Five-Point Program. This blueprint is flexible. I'll show you how to use the program for specific kinds of change such as breaking problem habits, achieving emotional growth, reducing stress, and changing careers. I'll also teach you how to adapt the program when your interests change. Finally, I'll help you identify the inner change blockers that stop so many of us from changing successfully, and give you proven ways to overcome the blocks.

TECHNIQUES, STRATEGIES, AND MYTHS

Throughout the book I'll show you the methods I have shared with aspiring changers through the years. I have included only the methods that have been the most successful for the greatest number of people. These methods are divided into two types—techniques and strategies. The techniques tend to be short, easy to remember, and quick to apply. Each should help you put change opportunities into perspective, and you can readily use them again and again. The strategies are often a bit more complicated, and may require your full attention. These are long-term actions for change. Together, the techniques and strategies integrate the best of both your logic and intuition, as you use your mind *and* your senses for positive change. I will also discuss several change myths that may stand in your way, and show you how to free yourself from their shadowy influence.

Let's not waste time, but begin our journey toward change right away.

THE PATH OF CHANGE

Picture yourself strolling along the well-worn path of your life into the woods. The woods are dark, and except for a distant glow of light that comes from a place beyond the trail, you see only images and shadows. The trail has a handrail that you grasp for security.

Grabbing this rail has obvious advantages: You don't get scratched by bushes and brambles, you don't trip on unseen roots and vines, and, above all, you don't get lost in the woods. But staying on the beaten path has a big downside too: You can go only where the trail leads you and the largest part of the forest remains inaccessible. You learn nothing about the lore of the woods or about survival by walking a narrow path, and you have little evidence that the path goes anywhere except in a circle.

Every so often the trail washes out. This will happen throughout your life, often in unexpected ways: the loss of a job, a forced relocation, a divorce, a serious illness, a new love, the birth of a child, or sudden and unexpected success. You can't escape stress even when you have been holding onto the rail for dear life.

As you move along the beaten path, you become aware of the rumblings of distant drums calling from mysterious places. Although the darkness looks worrisome, your curiosity and desire beckon you, so you let go of the rail and walk toward a promising new set of experiences.

Like many before you, you let go of the rail with apprehension only to discover that you can see more than before. Because of this, you feel a sensation of giddy liberation. Nonetheless, when you meet your first big challenge, you may feel like a butterfly in a hurricane. You long to return to the security of the well-worn path. Yet by sticking it out—learning to learn, adapting to change—you empower yourself to go forward.

You break from the rail when you test your skills in different ways. The shy person who socializes develops confidence. The procrastinator who gets organized discovers an inner drive for closure. The impulsive person who learns to reflect develops tolerance. Through this process, you command your finest attributes.

Changing paths involves some risk. The path you are on might be the very place you want to be. The new direction you choose can exclude other opportunities. Yet, when you feel as if you are going around in circles, prudent risks are normally worth taking. There is another reason to break from the rail. Looking back on their lives, most people regret what they did *not* dare to do more than they regret the errors they made. Those who rarely risk anything have the most to regret.

THE FIVE STAGES OF CHANGE

The story of the rail by the path describes critical elements in the decision to change. Important changes such as choosing a new career direction, building a relationship, or kicking a problem habit often involve time and risk. But what happens when you let go of the rail? Once you make the decision about a shift in direction, you are likely to pass through several stages as you change. These stages are awareness, action, assimilation, acceptance, and actualization.

1. **Awareness** almost always comes first. Successful change beings when you become aware of the thoughts, actions, and feelings that are your deepest resources, and those that are holding you back. Focusing on a specific problem helps you see changes you would best make in yourself. You may not yet have the information to follow through effectively, but when you achieve this awareness you have started the process of change.

2. **Action** begins when you commit to mentally prepare yourself to experiment with the planned change. You may start to prepare yourself by gathering information to fill important gaps in your knowledge. But there is more to this stage than gathering information. This phase involves taking real steps forward. It may take a lot of energy, since you will frequently have to fight against inertia and face unpleasant feelings of uncertainty and resistance.

3. **Assimilation** is the stage in which you see the connection between your aspirations, your self-concept, your beliefs, your feelings, and your actions. You begin to integrate the old with the new as you reshape your perspective. The desired change is at hand, but is not yet stable.

4. **Acceptance** comes as you work to stabilize the degree of change you have already achieved. Relapses are common, but these relapses are not failures. It often takes time and effort to consolidate gains. So you refuse to remain discouraged and you push yourself to bounce back. You accept this ebbing and flowing of change as normal and as a reflection of your human condition. If you fall back because you did not put enough determination and effort into changing or maintaining the change, you might wisely acknowledge that you are not a bad person simply because you fell

short of the mark. Instead, you can try again, perhaps with a new strategy.

5. Actualization is something you realize after the desired change has happened. It occurs when you absorb yourself in what you do and stretch your real strengths without second-guessing yourself. The changes you made along the way stabilize because of your initiative and the importance you place on developing yourself.

You may experience these stages of change in different ways many times over your life. You may move backwards. You may skip a stage. Assimilation, acceptance, and actualization may stay temptingly out of reach. Of the changes you can make, some will be evolutionary. Like a good spaghetti sauce, they require an abundance of ingredients and time to simmer. But to make meaningful changes in your life, you preferably begin with an awareness of what you are doing.

POSTSCRIPT

No one is immune to change. In life, change takes place each nanosecond. Nothing on this earth is safe from this continuous process. Even your environment can change from being nurturing to hostile.

Changes that happen around you and to you come in different forms. Some you love, feel drawn to, and try to speed up. You need time to adjust to other changes. Some you never get used to. Like Chinese water torture, you can take a few drops but more seem insufferable. When you hate a change, you are likely to equate it with horror, recoil from it, and try to stop it. Even when you have decided to make a positive change in your life, the experience can bring mixed feelings.

To achieve the change you want, you first realize that you have dependable inner resources to draw on to navigate through every stage of change, no matter how difficult it may seem. The next chapter shows you ways to broaden your perspective so that you can achieve the awareness that you need to continue your journey.

2

Broadening Your Perspective

Dan rarely went far from his home on his own. If he traveled more than a mile away, he would panic. He would experience heart palpitations, shortness of breath, and a raw unspeakable dread. Because of this phobia, he believed he would have a difficult time getting a college education, finding a good job, and experiencing romance. He felt helpless and hopeless. He wanted to get over his pessimism and fear, but he did not know how.

After I heard Dan's story I asked him to tell me more about his phobia. Did he remember when he first experienced these feelings? Dan gradually remembered a picnic he and his mother went on when he was six years old. He wandered off into the woods and got lost. He panicked. Then he heard his mother calling for him. He ran through the woods toward her voice. When he saw her arms open to welcome him, he felt enormous relief, and he felt safe.

When he connected the origins of his phobia with his present behavior, Dan gained a perspective on his problem. He could look back with a sympathetic understanding of how he had felt as a frightened six-year-old, and he could see clearly how and why the experience generalized to the present. He saw how fear gave way to relief when he felt protected, and thus why he continued to seek protection to feel secure. He also saw a behavior pattern where his fears caused him to dodge whatever felt uncomfortable.

Although this insight did not completely solve his problem, it was a crucial first step. Phobias lose power when the person recognizes and nullifies the thoughts and images that stimulate the panic. Dan learned to do this. Over time he changed his phobic outlook to one of self-confidence and began to travel freely.

THE POWER OF PERSPECTIVE

Dan's case shows how powerful perspective can be in influencing your feelings and actions. It illustrates that a person's views of reality change as perspective changes.

Getting a clear picture of what is going on inside and around you, as Dan did, is the next step in your journey of self-discovery. As the English poet John Milton wrote in *Paradise Lost*, "The mind has its own place and in itself can make a heav'n of hell and a hell of heav'n."

In order to open your mind to positive change, you need to develop what I call a *rational perspective*. This means that you learn to look at yourself and your world with a logical eye, unencumbered by myths and needless fears.

BUILDING A RATIONAL PERSPECTIVE

Building a rational perspective involves putting failure into perspective, confronting any beliefs that are holding us back, and looking beyond our superficial symptoms to the true source of our problems. Let's look at how to approach each of these steps.

Put Failure Into Perspective

People who are afraid of failure struggle against change because they lack the confidence in themselves to manage the unknown without certainty and guarantees. Therefore, it is important to put failure into a different perspective as a prelude to change.

If you are trying to escape from a deadly enemy, failure has serious consequences. Failures that result from our attempts to master our world, however, are rarely fatal. Nevertheless, failure is a deflating experience. Thinking yourself a "failure" or being called a "failure" is belittling, like being labeled a "dud," an "incompetent loser." Because of these degrading associations, the possibility of failure causes many to hesitate to try something new or even to take reasonable risks.

There is another reason many of us hesitate before starting something new. Challenges that involve uncertainty often evoke fear and discomfort. Even when this fear is mild, it can distort our outlook and water down our confidence.

How would you like to drop "failure" from your functional vocabulary and rid yourself of this self-defeating fear? To accomplish this goal, teach yourself to see your change efforts as experiments. You can do this by pretending to work as an applied scientist. A scientist or engineer tests many promising ideas in the process of finding solutions for challenging problems, realizing that many trials may be needed before success. Thomas Edison, for example, tried thousands of filaments for the electric light before he found one that worked. As months turned to years, not even one filament lasted more than two seconds. Finally he discovered the one that would give light for an acceptable time before burning out. As one experiment after another ended in failure, he didn't tell himself, "My God, I made a mistake. I'd better stop now." As Edison saw it, he did not make even one mistake! At every step he discovered something valid—that a particular filament would not work. Indeed, he saw the process not as a series of failures, but as a single experiment that happened to require thousands of steps.

The power of this example is not that if you have the patience of a saint you can make worthy discoveries. After all, how many of us really want to be saints? Instead, by seeing your constructive actions as enlightening—no matter whether they result in what you hoped for or in something else—you can then press forward knowing you are willing to risk error.

Edison's experimental approach will give you many joys of accomplishment. Still, many times you will face discouragement and feel frustration. Why is that? When you take steps to learn, discover, and create, you have no guarantee you won't stumble. The experimental process is like learning to read. You start at your readiness level and build competence as you read more challenging books. Once you read well, your world opens to endless possibilities.

Remember—error is an inevitable part of life. That is why pencils have erasers on them. Most everyday errors are manageable provided you act like a problem solver. From this perspective, you see that making mistakes is understandable and, more importantly, that the *essence of you* remains acceptable even when you make a series of mistakes. Now you can convincingly take the position that there is no failure; there are only experiments that prove productive to a lesser or a greater degree.

When you put failure into perspective and view life as an experiment, you set the action stage into motion and open the possibility of gaining valuable insights. How does abandoning failure lead to insightfulness? Psychologist Wolfgang Kohler (1925) gives us a partial answer. Kohler conducted an experiment whereby he put a banana outside a chimpanzee's cage just beyond the hungry animal's reach. He also placed a stick in the cage. Before long, the chimp made an important connection. As though a light bulb had gone on in its head, the animal grabbed the stick and used it to pull in the banana. If it did not get the banana, the chimp would feel frustrated *but not disgraced*. Embarrassment associated with failure is a human concern.

Kohler demonstrated that insight arises from necessity. Still, there is another side to this story. His chimps grew up in environments where they occasionally played with sticks. If one repeats the experiment with chimps reared in captivity but without stick experience, the animals do not make the connection and don't get the banana. This variable suggests that unless you get a variety of new experiences, you may have few productive insights.

To widen the range of your constructive experiences, consider putting aside fear of failure, and start experimenting.

Challenge Your Beliefs

Since the catalyst for change lies in broadening your perspective, challenging your beliefs plays a prime role in any self-change. Your beliefs are those convictions that you take for truth. They strongly influence your outlook, emotions, and actions.

Once adopted, beliefs can be very powerful—so powerful that they can either nourish or rot the roots of a culture. As logician and psychologist Alexander Bain wrote in 1859, "The great master fallacy of the human mind is believing too much." Yet false beliefs are tough to change, even when we discover facts that point to a radically different direction. For example, if you believed that all people are selfish and only look out for themselves, would you change your opinion if strangers—say, in a natural disaster such as a flood or fire—risked their lives to save yours? Or would you attribute their actions to self-serving motivations such as a desire to be seen as a hero or receive a reward?

You can feel the power of even a trivial belief when you are faced with a solid fact that proves it wrong. Suppose an acquaintance asks you to give your opinion about Washington Street. You believe the street is in the crime-riddled north end of town. You comment that you'd rather not live near that street and no more is said. Several weeks later, you are driving through the south end of town—the high-income district—and see Washington Street. You can't believe your eyes but can't deny that the sign says Washington Street. You still might "feel" that the street is on the north end of town even though you know it isn't. You feel uncomfortable, like something is incomplete.

Beliefs have enormous power. People have fought bloody wars over religious beliefs, and continue to do so. The same is true for political-ideological beliefs and notions of ethnic superiority.

Beliefs can even prevail over instincts for self-preservation. In battle, for instance, soldiers take enormous personal risk because of strongly held beliefs about the goodness of their side and the depravity of the people on the other. Under these conditions, people may short-circuit their survival instincts.

We lose many good opportunities and make many needless mistakes when we hew to unfounded but destructive beliefs. For example:

- If you think your mate is an unfaithful scoundrel, you will feel differently about people who believe their mates are trustworthy.

- If you believe everyone is out to get you, you may antagonize the majority who are not.

- If you believe you cannot change, you will not.

You must be willing to face your beliefs and test them against the facts if you intend to broaden your perspective. By testing your beliefs, you can show yourself that the world may not be as static as you once thought.

Uproot Your Symptoms

If you believe your problem is something like anxiety, depression, compulsive behavior, or procrastination, you may have limited your perspective. Limiting perspective limits progress. Anxiety, depression, compulsions, and procrastination are symptoms. But of what? These and other psychological symptoms, such as fear of change (neophobia), often mask destructive beliefs such as self-doubts and discomfort fears.

Dealing with problems or symptoms, though, is not an either–or choice. There is no need to ignore the symptom if overcoming that symptom is the path to change. If your symptom is an elevator phobia and you work on the ninety-fifth floor of a building, you could try to desensitize yourself to that fear. Begin by first walking on, then off, the elevator at the first floor. When you feel comfortable, elevate to the second floor and then return to the first. When you have gotten this far, repeat the process at successively higher floors until you reach the ninety-fifth floor or above. You also can mentally "reframe" the situation. Think of the elevator as a protective shell. With this image, the elevator may appear friendly. By following these approaches, you are conquering your symptoms.

You can build durable self-confidence by working directly at uprooting problem symptoms. To start:

- Figure out what you are thinking, imagining, or telling yourself that distresses you. Consider whether your present beliefs grow from assumptions or fact. Check these thoughts out to see if you can prove or disprove them.

- Examine your most valuable resources and decide which of them can override the symptom. Your resources may include clear thinking, tolerance, relaxation, a gift for strategy, persistence, openness, and the ability to profit from information and wise suggestions. Now, can you find alternate ways to solve the problem?

- Strengthen your valuable resources by exercising them. Simulate problems and then deal with the simulation. Act out what you want to say and do in your mind. Finally, test your resources out on real-life situations.

The Stepping-out-of-Character Technique

You can begin to build a rational perspective by stepping out of character. You step out of character whenever you experiment with new ways of thinking and behaving.

Let's take a common problem—fear of change—to see how you can use the stepping-out-of-character technique to discover hidden qualities about yourself. (What is a problem for one person may be a challenge or a joy for another. So the following examples for how to step out of character may suit some readers but not others. The important part is to pick something that is out of character for *you*.)

If you habitually wear drab clothing, you can step out of character by wearing attractive, brightly colored clothing. If you wear brightly colored clothing, try wearing something neutral.

You can add variety and fun to this stepping-out-of-character project by exercising your imagination. Go to a restaurant for breakfast. If you see listed on the menu "two eggs, any style," calmly ask for one fried and one scrambled egg. Then order coffee and quietly sip it through a straw. If you wish, order tea and ask for a warm cup. Go to a shoe store and test a pair of sneakers by jogging in place.

If you are normally quiet in public, try speaking up during the question-and-answer period at a conference. If you normally dominate a conversation, be quiet and listen and see what you can learn. If you regularly take a "right to life" position on abortion, work up a "pro-choice" argument. This may help you develop empathy for the values others hold, and this empathy can add a quietly persuasive quality when you express your real views.

As you practice this technique, you may feel your discomforts fade and find that you can now accomplish what you once viewed as difficult. You will develop your rational perspective to the point that you can make many small changes. You can then apply your new tool to the task of achieving larger changes.

USING YOUR RATIONAL PERSPECTIVE TO COMBAT CHANGE MYTHS

Now that you have seen how to build a rational perspective, let's look at how you can use it. Many of us embrace myths that narrow our perspective on change. If you suspect that your perspective is distorted by one or more of the following twelve myths, imagine your rational perspective having an engaging debate with the myth. Repeat this debate until your rational perspective stays at the forefront of your thoughts and shapes your perspective.

1. *The "swept with the tide" myth:* Here people think that cosmic forces control their destinies. They believe they can't stop predestined events because all our lives are mapped out from the moment of our birth. This myth, that our destinies lie in the position of the stars, is more deterministic than the "Que será será" view, which holds that all events unfold naturally. Instead, when you hew to a "swept with the tide" view, you believe you can play no active part in what unfolds. Paradoxically, you may look for an oracle to tell you what is in store for you, hoping you can avoid catastrophe.

   Rational perspective: You govern your life through your dispositions, aptitudes, knowledge, and perceptions. You have the power of choice to change from within. Choice means that you can decide how and when and where you pilot yourself through the channels of life. Thus, many events in life come about through your design. For instance, you decide what course of study you'll follow. You decide what you will do for recreation.

2. *The "divine spirit" myth:* When you are hung up with this belief, you figure that change happens in mysterious and magical ways. A divine spirit or kindly person will guide you to paradise. You need only accept these cosmic influences to feel charged for change.

   Rational perspective: While the idea that you change through the efforts of a mysterious helper is appealing, don't count on a divine spirit to materialize and magically revolutionize your life. For an alternative, consider that you become empowered as a result of your independent action.

3. *The "demoniacal influence" myth:* This is the sinister twin of the divine spirit myth. It holds that we are powerless to influence our future because we collapse under the authority of ominous powers. Excuses dominate reality: "The Devil made me do it." "It was the booze." "I have a compulsion that I can't resist."

   Rational perspective: You are not to blame for your proclivities, but you are responsible for your acts. You have the ability to override destructive proclivities and add interest and quality to your life.

4. *The "good things happen to good people and bad things happen to bad people" myth:* This notion that people get their just due grows from another belief, that there is fairness in the universe. One need only wait for justice.

   Rational perspective: This is fairy tale logic. Good and evil are value terms. The universe could care less about morality. Many considered Mikoyan to be as evil as Stalin, and he survived to an old age to die of natural causes. More people we might consider "good" suffered and died under Hitler than did those we'd consider "bad." Catastrophes happen to everyone.

5. *The "incubator" myth:* You can change if, and only if, you have the support and encouragement of others. You must

ask for, then wait for, people to help. Without this support, you will make meager progress. The incubator myth is the foundation beneath those twelve-step programs that teach dependency.

Rational perspective: Although warmth and support are desirable, what happens if no one shows up? People with pioneering spirit stick it out to produce change on their own volition and in their own way. You are resourceful and can put this pioneering ability to work with or without other people. Although some advice and support may help, you choose how you will change and how you will act on your own volition. As the architect of your inner change, you decide what support helps you, and you can choose not to become addicted to support to the point where you develop an anguishing dependency on a group or individual.

6. *The "automatic change" myth:* If you can see the need for a change, you can change by issuing an intellectual command. The decision should be a sufficient catalyst for action.

Rational perspective: You progress when you replace a harmful habit with a constructive one. Don't expect permanent change to come about just because you decide it should happen. In most cases, self-change requires extensive and focused efforts. Instead of issuing edicts to yourself, get specific about the type of change you want, and what you can do. Then concentrate your efforts on making the change you had in mind. The efforts that follow can stimulate improvement faster than an intellectual demand.

7. *The "change requires preparation" myth:* The only way you can change is through advanced preparation. There is no room for experimentation and serendipity.

Rational perspective: There is no hard and fast rule for when or how to start a change. Sometimes preparation for change involves incubation. At other times, the preparation for change is change itself. For example, you don't learn to play golf well simply by reading or watching the game. You have to get out there and swing a club. Over-preparation leads to analysis paralysis—endless study and preparation without change.

8. *The "analyst's circle" myth:* Our real motives have roots in the past and in our unconscious. We have no choice but to repeat past mistakes because our unconscious motivations drive our present actions.

   Rational perspective: Many of us repeat self-defeating patterns such as wrongfully putting ourselves down for no good reason at all. However, we can change these patterns. We first become aware of how we limit ourselves when we listen to our inner voices and link their meaning to our feelings and actions. If we don't like the results of our thoughts and actions, we can learn ways to change our thinking and acting. The "analyst's circle" myth leads to action paralysis: You can't act until you've solved the mystery of your existence.

9. *The "unyielding habit" myth:* We are creatures of habit and routine from which we cannot break free. It is our destiny to follow these patterns throughout our lives.

   Rational perspective: Some habits and routines have functional value; others do not. We are a species of habit, but because we can contemplate, we also are creatures of change. Thus you can choose to make a change for the better. You can take the first step to supplant an unprofitable habit with a rewarding one whenever you choose. When you change your actions you can change even the most harmful habits.

10. *The "empty box" myth:* We are a collection of specialized reflexes that respond adaptively to changing stimuli. The pains and pleasures of life shape our responses and our fate.

    Rational perspective: Fear can be freezing and pleasure enveloping, so we seek pleasure and avoid pain. Not all pleasure is constructive, though. We are more than a bundle of reflexes; we have the ability to separate the constructive pleasure from the destructive pleasure. We can choose and make changes that benefit us. For example, everyday many people give up "pleasure giving" drugs, alcohol, and tobacco permanently because they look beyond their noses, decide to stop, and then quit.

11. *The "change is beyond reach" myth:* Change is so difficult as to be either impossible or not worth the effort to achieve.

    Rational perspective: Change is an abstraction until anchored to a particular set of goals and actions. Look at the goals, steps, and results. What steps do you need to take? Can you leapfrog to where you want to go? People who hold to this view automatically quit before they begin. Change becomes the impossible task. The cliché "Why bother, I can't do anything right anyway" comes from people who have chosen this path. This attitude of mind reflects a depressed state. A prime remedy for depression is activity: Challenge this myth by taking small steps toward an achievable change.

12. *The "Volga boatman" myth:* People with this outlook see themselves endlessly toiling and laboring without hope for relief or change. The weary housewife, tired laborer, and burned-out healer belong in this class. They see their tasks as a daily drudgery often with worthy purpose, but with no end in sight. Change is beyond reach. Yet, there is a vague hope for freedom at the end of the trail—retirement, heaven.

    Rational perspective: Rather than waiting for the end of life to find your just reward, consider the opposite: You can make your work and life into fun. You can leave the Volga boat by applying your efforts to constructive results. If you feel as if you are pulling the same boat up and down stream, you can change your philosophy to encompass the view that you have choices and that you can exercise those choices and find relief from repetitious, burdensome tasks.

You've probably noticed that some myths contradict others. The myths of automatic change and of change requiring preparation are at the opposite ends of a dimension. People have a wide range of attitudes that inhibit positive, purposeful change. Whatever myth blocks your path, however, a rational perspective can help combat it.

POSTSCRIPT

We look at the outside world from the inside. Thus each person's perspective will have a decidedly personal tone. Because we are normally more familiar with what is going on inside than outside, the information we take in registers through various filters: We prefer to see what we want to see and, unsurprisingly, normally see things our way. Our perspectives are just that—our perspectives.

Our perspective on change is everchanging. Change circles everything we do. One theory cannot fit all conditions. The rules of change practically always have exceptions. Nevertheless, you can change to become a more knowledgeable, perceptive, assertive, warm, venturesome, tolerant, self-confident, and adaptable you. You can develop your desirable qualities by putting change actions into motion and by measuring them against experience. If you don't like the results, you change your actions.

Now that we've worked on and changed how we see outside events, it's time to move on to how we see ourselves.

3

Looking Within

It was a nightmare. Robert tumbled out of control across a cold damp plain of jagged rocks. Then the rocks changed into death-gray faces with long, hooked noses and twisted teeth. Next, he saw this ghastly crowd pointing at him. In shrill whining voices, they cast accusations at him: "You'll never amount to anything." "No woman will ever love you." Then the faces disappeared.

When Robert awoke, his head felt like an open canyon with voices reverberating from the past: "You're no good." "You're a loser." "People hate you." "You can't do anything right." "You never finish anything you start." "You can't control yourself." "You're a fake."

As he discussed this, Robert began to realize that these thoughts felt like the dream. He thought, "Perhaps there is a connection."

Robert gradually came to realize that he was the author of the voices in his dream. This led him to think, "If I am the author of my dreams, I also am the author of my most beleaguering daytime thoughts. As the author, I can change this script."

Robert's case vividly illustrates the importance of how we see ourselves. Our self-concept is critical to how we think, what we do, the type of changes we make, and how we feel about ourselves.

Indeed, the quality and direction of the changes we make depend significantly on how we look at ourselves and who we think we are. In this chapter, we'll consider what goes into a self-concept and examine some ways to improve it.

THE SIGNIFICANCE OF SELF-CONCEPT

Who you are—more precisely, your self-concept—is central to the quality of your internal change, because this view governs the way you see much of your life.

Your self-concept is not static. You can feel inferior one hour and brimming with confidence the next. The changes take place because of your mood, circumstances, and what you happen to be thinking about at the time. Indeed, you have many different perceptions about yourself, and these perceptions can be influenced by situation. You might, for instance, feel like a klutz at a party and thereby be uncomfortable introducing yourself to new people. On the other hand, you can brim with confidence when you play tennis. You can feel inferior when you deal with a boisterous co-worker and feel bright and contributory when you work for a boss who genuinely appreciates your efforts and contributions.

Conversely, your self-concept is also relatively stable. Like gravity, it pulls your views of events and yourself to a core of ideas you have about yourself. Contradictions are a common part of everyone's psychic life.

Your self-concept is part of a complex web of often-contradictory ideas and beliefs. When you have a fairly stable but positive self-concept, you will find that you adapt effectively to changing conditions. With a consistently negative self-concept, you will have an extremely restricted sense of self. You will normally experience little variance in your outlook about yourself. Occasionally you may feel great when something works out, but this cloak on your misguided sense of worthlessness is only temporary.

Your dominant thoughts about yourself are persistent. Thus people who see themselves as "losers" will still think of themselves as losers even if they have a great job, marry well by anyone's definition, and win the top prize on "Jeopardy."

Negative self-concepts are normally persistent because they resist change. A negative self-concept reveals itself as a self-disapproving state of mind, such as the notion that if you fail at anything you try, you're a failure, plain and simple. You may even believe you are uniquely the most inept and lowly faker who ever lived. If you dwell on disapproving of yourself in this way, your soft emotions of warmth, compassion, and empathy rarely do more than make cameo appearances.

People who suffer from these inadequate self-images will normally attribute their success to mere luck, will secretly feel that their mates must be fools for staying with them, or will find other means to explain away fortunate events as something other than what they are. So great is the power of the sense of identity—and the terror of losing it, no matter how disagreeable—that untold millions inflict needless misery on themselves and others for no rational reason at all.

At the core of this fear of loss of identity is a fear of losing control. Your very sense of reality—your ability to distinguish, say, between dreaming and waking—may be at risk when you feel a threat to your sense of identity. Yet, you can change your self-concept for the better without the slightest risk that you will stop being who you are or that you will lose any of the control you actually have. The only identity you'll lose is a set of ideas you don't really want anyway: erroneous beliefs about your chance of progress and misapprehensions about who you are and about your chances for success.

Because your self-concept is uniquely important to what you do, let's look at key elements that go into that self-definition.

This self-concept of yours includes stable traits such as shyness, intelligence, and introversion or extroversion that often appear shortly after birth and influence what you do and, in part, how others respond to you. If you feel introverted, you'll normally spend more time dealing with ideas and objects than will the extroverted person. These preset tendencies influence the types and quality of your experiences. Still, you develop your self-concept through experience and your interpretations of the roles you play. Because you learn your self view in the first place, you can change it through education.

The essential elements of a healthy self-concept include frustration tolerance, self-image, self-acceptance, self-esteem, self-efficacy, and self-control.

- *Frustration tolerance* is the willingness to accept unpleasant experiences and feelings. This acceptance requires the ability to delay gratification, to interpose reason between impulse and action, and to maintain self-control in trying circumstances. High frustration tolerance develops alongside of persistence, self-control, and accomplishment.

- Your *self-image* relates to the picture you believe you project to the outside world. It includes the roles you play: wise person, beautiful princess, warrior, protector, teacher, clown, or gadfly. Your self-image is how you believe others think of you.

- *Self-acceptance* is an attitude of mind that says, "For better or for worse, I'm the only me I can be."

- *Self-esteem* means that you feel that your acts are worthy, in your eyes if not in other's.

- *Self-efficacy* is psychologist Albert Bandura's (1982, 1986, 1990) way of describing people's beliefs in their ability to exercise control over events that affect their own lives. With high self-efficacy you believe your acts have impact on the world you inhabit—that your behavior makes a difference. This potent belief regulates your motivations and actions and the constructive changes you make. The opposite of self-efficacy is helplessness.

- *Self-control* is an orderly and organized approach to life's challenges and problems. Management consultant Peter Drucker teaches that the greatest intellectual wisdom, knowledge, and information are useless unless converted to actions and products. This output is a measure of effectiveness, which is "getting the right things done." Without self-discipline and self-control, the right things don't get done or don't get done well.

These six ingredients—along with other attributes such as values, aptitudes, moods, illusions, attitudes, and beliefs—make up your self-concept. It is by developing these six parts of your self-concept that you build a solid sense of self. Just as with the change process, self-concept reconstruction starts with *awareness* of what you want to develop, followed by self-controlled *action*, which leads to *assimilation, acceptance,* and *actualization* of self.

BUILDING A SOLID SELF-CONCEPT

Imagine that you've entered a fascinating room filled with valuable objects and unnecessary clutter. The room dances with shadows.

Through the haze you see many pictures and books that promise interesting stories. As your eyes dart about the room, you see many possibilities. So you decide to change parts of the room to make it a better place for you to live.

First you clean the windows and clear away the clutter. Now the floors look dingy, so you clean and wax them. Then you paint the walls. You add furniture, plants, and rugs to complement the pictures and stories and to bring all the elements together. Each day you find a new way to maintain and improve this room of yours. This is your room; it is like no other.

If you choose to use your resources well and realize the potential of your room, you are likely to follow practices that effective people typically employ. They analyze, plan, organize, and implement. They show cognitive flexibility, which is the ability to evaluate situations as they are happening; to see their part in the process; and to act, correct, or change when necessary in order to bring about a productive result that is in line with their goals.

Just as you fulfilled the potential of your room, you can create an inner world that is richly you. You can experience the ecstasy of accomplishment. In other words, you can build a strong and healthy self-concept. To build a solid self-concept, you should first understand that your identity is not the same thing as the sum of your actions. Thus, you are smart to avoid rating your *self* according to your actions. However, with that in mind, understand that you are still responsible for evaluating what you do and accepting the consequences of your actions.

Know Who You Are Not

Let's examine some views that support the powerful idea that you are more than just what you do. We'll also look at other ideas that can lead you to a negative set of conclusions about yourself.

You may measure your value as a person by such external factors as your accomplishments, wealth, and status. These measures can reflect your self-efficacy. But in some cases, people with long lists of accomplishments and advantages disparage themselves, because they envy others with more, or because they believe they have not done enough.

There are obvious advantages to having accomplishments. It's nice to feel positive about these results. The *big lie* comes into play when you believe that if you don't perform great feats and achieve prominence or lead a perfect life, you are an inferior person.

The definition of personal worthiness varies from culture to culture, but the majority believe that each of us would be wise to do the best we can and to reach for excellence whenever we can, within the time we have available.

This "do the best you can" philosophy has a hopeful ring. When you strive for excellence, you continually stretch to develop your resources and to produce constructive results. You don't waste your energy in a futile pursuit of perfection.

Striving for excellence and demanding perfection are unrelated. One is possible, the other impossible. Perfectionism is a symptom of distress. Striving for excellence is a way to control the events that affect your life.

Now let's get back to the "you are more than your actions" idea. Consider this: You can't legitimately define your entire essence based on a single character trait or action! This is the heart of the self-concept theory developed by pioneering psychologist Albert Ellis. Here is a synthesis of his position: Realize that you are not stupid just because you did a stupid thing. Nor, by the way, are you smart just because you solved one tough problem, brave just because you performed a courageous act yesterday, or good just because you have a compulsion to help people. Your self just is. Your self is not good or bad, brave or cowardly, dumb or smart. We add existential depth to this theory through adding the concept of values.

What is real and what exists for people are the values they create to guide their conduct. These values include their sense of responsibility and the freedom they gain through the choices they make. (I discuss values in more depth in Chapter 4.)

Avoid Rating Yourself

Your self-concept comes partially from a natural tendency to rate yourself. Although this tendency is very influential, it does not create a full picture of the self.

It is normal and often useful to make comparisons. We measure championship efforts by comparing the results of performance. Unfortunately, some of us turn this natural tendency against ourselves by matching our performances to unreachable Utopian standards and then debasing our worth when we realize that we cannot measure up to them.

People who follow this pattern often suffer from *comparativitis*. Like a virus that infects the body, comparativitis affects the mind. Comparativitis victims routinely spy on themselves and infect themselves with thoughts of unworthiness. When you fall into this trap, try comparing yourself to individuals with severe physical or mental limitations. If you come out ahead, does this mean you are more worthy and wonderful? Does winning this comparison improve the quality of your life? No. This analysis shows only that you have advantages in some areas over certain individuals.

In the same way, it is pointless to base your sense of worth on Utopian standards. Consider that when Sir Thomas More wrote about Utopia in 1516, he described its location as "nowhere." Forget about finding the Utopia of perfection; it exists only in your mind. Instead, put your energy into bringing your cherished and rich visions to life.

The following worth index, lifeline, spot, and jug of coins techniques are different ways I have used to help clients avoid rating their worth. Try them and see if they help you build this aspect of your self-concept.

THE WORTH INDEX TECHNIQUE

Imagine trying to accurately define your worth by adding up all of your "plus" and "minus" traits and actions and coming up with a sum total. Could you accurately do this? Probably not! You would find many complications. For example, can you value all "plus" and "minus" qualities equally?

In theory you could assign higher numerical values to your more desirable traits and qualities and assign lower values to others. You could rate each of your thoughts and actions. You could use an electronic spreadsheet to calculate a number to describe your worthiness index. Still, this measurement technique would prove arduous to use because you would need to continue to upgrade the rating as new experiences developed. That's why you'd need an electronic spreadsheet to "automatically" recalculate the changing numbers. Because worth is not an all-or-none affair, you also would find that you have changing degrees of worthiness. Through this exhausting exercise, you can prove to yourself that it is untenable to give yourself one global self-worth rating that can endure for all time.

THE LIFELINE TECHNIQUE

Let's use the idea of a lifeline to add another perspective to this problem. Imagine a line that moves through time and space from your birth to your death. This is your lifeline. Thousands of your qualities, character traits, and skills as well as millions of your thoughts, feelings, actions, and memories rotate around this ever-extending line. In existential terms, this is the sum total of you to date.

If you hold to a consistently unfavorable self-view, you will tend to see only those fragments of your lifeline that support that view. To maintain your negative self-concept, you will need to exclude positive events. You also will need to define your worthiest qualities and accomplishments as random events—mere accidents that just happened by chance along the way.

You don't have to stick with such undermining thinking. Whenever you think poorly of yourself, think about your long life-line. Ask yourself how any action, trait, or pattern of behavior can make you totally good or bad, lazy or enterprising, brilliant or foolish. When you match a single unfortunate action—or a group of them—against the millions of your advantageous actions and qualities, how do they all balance out?

THE SPOT TECHNIQUE

Take a moment to ask yourself how you feel when you make a mistake. Do you feel that making mistakes shows that you're an incompetent bumbler? Can you see that this view makes self-efficacy unattainable? Can you imagine that it's possible to both make mistakes and still feel pleased about yourself?

The spot technique can help you put making mistakes into perspective. To use this method, look at your favorite work of art. Try to find a flaw. (Or a less-than-beautiful section—say, the nostrils on the "Mona Lisa"!) Once you have the flaw in mind, ask yourself, "Would I throw out this work of art because of the defect?" Chances are you wouldn't. Chances are you would see that the picture as a whole is still beautiful.

Now consider one of your less-than-desirable actions. Maybe you forgot to pay your phone bill or you screamed at your employer and lost your job. Admit that you goofed and then ask yourself how these transgressions really diminish your essence. Is it not possible to enjoy the whole of you with "flaws" while you work to change what displeases you?

THE JUG OF COINS TECHNIQUE

Let's look at the idea that you are more than your actions in a different way. The jug of coins technique shows that you have qualities of both greater and lesser value and that you don't have to rate yourself only on the basis of your least-valued qualities.

Imagine that you have a jug filled with thousands of old and new coins of different denominations. A few are rare and priceless. Some are ordinary. A few are slugs. The person with a positive self-view accepts the different coins as a part of the self. The person with a prevailing negative self-concept puts a magnifying glass over the slugs, and that is all that individual normally sees.

Consider: Would you throw out all the coins because the ordinary coins lie alongside the more valued ones or the jug contains a few slugs? When you apply this idea to your self-concept, consider whether you should give up on yourself because of the "slugs" in your life or emphasize getting better use of your valuable coins.

DO RATE YOUR ACTIONS

You are not your actions, but you can still rate them! If you study hard to pass a test and do brilliantly, you can give a high rating to the way you studied, as well as to the result. If you like the rating, repeat the actions that produced the result. If you shoplift because you seek excitement, you'd wisely rate this behavior as poor. If you don't like the rating, you can teach yourself to behave in a different way.

Once you stop making sweeping self-evaluations, you will take emotional events—for example, being rejected by someone— seriously but will not let them devastate your self-concept.

Actions are worth rating. However, you don't have to be great at something to think well of yourself. You just have to decide to accept yourself, focus your efforts, and operate as effectively as you can.

The idea that you are not your actions raises hackles in many quarters. The complaint is that once we get away from the idea that bad people do bad deeds, we can't hold people responsible for raping, extorting, robbing, and murdering. The murderer will say, "Sure I killed Mama. That doesn't mean I'm a bad person. After all, I am not my actions, am I?" The response to the murderer must be: "No, you are not your actions. Still, you are going to prison because you are *accountable* for your actions."

That you are not your actions—and that you need not judge

your value as a person on that basis—in no way suggests that your rights have increased or that your responsibilities have diminished. It does mean that you can say to yourself, "I made a mistake," rather than "That mistake proves I'm worthless." Thus, you need not base your essence on a single action or pattern—however onerous, stupid, or illegal!

I cannot overstate the value of the "I am not my actions" philosophy. By separating your sense of self-worth from your prior conduct, you can avoid the error of resting on past laurels or dwelling on past failures. You can change unwelcome but repeated patterns of conduct without wasting your time berating yourself and repeating the conduct. Put your efforts into changing the behavior that got you into difficulty in the first place.

Once you accept that self-condemnation is an act of futility, the prospect of change is much less frightening. Indeed, it becomes something you can look forward to with pleasure.

The Attribution Technique

Make a chart with these five headings: Doing Things, Feeling Things, Personal Things, Interests, and Values. Under each heading, list your traits and qualities.

"Doing things" may include the ability to drive an automobile, read and write, do carpentry work, listen attentively, assert your point of view, plan, organize, paint a house, fix a computer. Include anything that involves skilled action.

"Feeling things" may include your ability to empathize or to feel sad, happy, jealous, compassionate, fearful, enthusiastic, hopeful, lonely, trusting, annoyed, curious, confident, desirable, disappointed, angry, frustrated, irritated, relaxed, guilty, ashamed. Use any words that describe your feelings.

"Personal things" can include your beliefs, opinions, and qualities, such as friendliness, seriousness, practicality, creativity, inventiveness, dominance, adaptability, warmth, reserve, intelligence. List words that describe yourself.

"Interests" can include art, sports, the outdoors, social activities, science, strategy games. Select items that describe what you like to do.

"Values" can include family, fairness, strength, trust, integrity, material goods, friendship. Choose terms that describe anything you consider important in your life.

From now on, whenever you block yourself from making a change because you label yourself inferior, ask yourself how a person like you with the varied attributes on your chart can be irreversibly inferior. True, some people may have attributes that are different from those of others. True, some others may have certain stronger resources. Yet these differences do not take anything away from your resources. You still have them. You can still use them.

The Question Technique

Here is another technique that will help you keep the stable and the changing elements of your self-concept in perspective. Ask yourself searching questions and find the truth through your responses.

The technique works best when you phrase the questions in answerable terms. Answerable questions contain the root of their own solution. A productive question such as "*What* do I tell myself about myself that stops me from expressing my opinions to my friends?" leads to a process of discovery and solution. If you suffer from a poor self-concept because you tell yourself you are no good, try asking yourself *how* your thousands of helpful talents and qualities fit with this "no good" self-view.

Not all questions, however, have meaningful answers. Vague, metaphysical questions such as "Why don't I have confidence in myself?" or "Why do bad things always happen to me?" can lead you to an impasse. This search for causes can prove self-defeating when the effort sidetracks you from asking questions that yield answers that lead to self-improvement.

Some "why" questions do get at issues. You might find it interesting, for example, to discover *why* the ancient Egyptian pharaohs built pyramids. On a personal level you ponder productively why you act in a certain way without turning the question against yourself (as in: "Why can't I . . . ?" or "Why don't I . . . ?"). Still, to avoid the risk of entering the realm of the metaphysical, you can rephrase such questions using a "what" format. What did the pharaohs believe they gained from building pyramids? What would you like to accomplish by testing new actions?

POSTSCRIPT

William Makepeace Thackeray wrote that "the world is like a looking glass and gives back to everyone the reflection of his face."

Most of what we do results from various habits of mind. One such habit is your self-concept. The way you overcome a distorted self-concept is to replace debilitating thoughts with constructive thinking and purposeful, constructive actions. This process takes thought, practice, and time. Be prepared to suffer relapses as you construct your self-concept. We change as we learn and learn as we change, and setbacks are the hallmarks of effort.

The value of a positive self-concept is that when you do something wrong, you don't have to declare yourself a rotten person. Instead, you can say to yourself, "I behaved poorly in that situation. I can change!"

Now we move on to examine values—a core element of self-discovery.

4

Shaping Your Values

Your basic values are key elements of change; they influence the quality of your choices and the worth of the changes you set in motion. Defining your values is a vital phase of self-change because if you know and shape your core values, you will have a clear sense of your change goals.

THE IMPORTANCE OF VALUES

Rules, procedures, rituals, folkways, mores, and laws guide many of your actions. You wait in your place in line. You respect your neighbor's property because you want your neighbor to respect your possessions. Values go beyond these structured rules of society—they are your *core beliefs* about what is right, worthy, good, or moral. They are the deeper structures of thought that guide your actions.

You organize your moral outlook around your values, and this organization of thought motivates and guides your action. These codes and standards sometimes involve abstract principles such as freedom. They include what you stand for. When you have no values, you stand for everything and nothing.

Higher-order values, such as friendship, justice, integrity, responsibility, or aesthetics, reflect what you do and how you feel. When you help a friend regain a lost right, you show that you value justice and friendship. When you appreciate a red sunrise on a spring morning, you show that you value beauty.

VALUE SYSTEMS

We organize our thinking around our values, and these themes help shape our perspective and actions. Thus, we admire or scorn people such as Mother Teresa, Sun Myung Moon (leader of the Unification church), Richard Nixon, Mark Twain, Mahatma Gandhi, Thomas Jefferson, Mao Tse-tung, or Adolf Hitler because of the values they represent.

Our values punctuate our purpose and positions on matters we consider highly important. That is why people with different value systems are not likely to agree. Imagine Hitler discussing his views of freedom with Thomas Jefferson! Think about Michelangelo and J. Paul Getty debating about the relative importance of aesthetics or politics and economics.

There are five common value systems: objective, subjective, humanistic, hedonistic, and everyday. These value systems have their own unique fingerprints and compasses for change. The more you know about each, the better you know how values motivate change.

I introduce these five general value systems with a value question asking what you would do if you were in a particular situation. Next I describe the value system the situation illustrates. Then I suggest an answer to the original question. You can compare my answer to your response and see if it is consistent with that value system.

Objective Values

You are arbitrating a dispute between your best friend and a person whose views you often contest. Your judgment will influence which person will get promoted to a higher-paying position.

You listen to both sides of the story and find that your friend is partially correct but mostly wrong. Her adversary is mostly correct but has trouble articulating her position. What do you do? The answer to this question may give you an insight into your objective value system.

The eighteenth-century French writer and philosopher Voltaire (Bestman et al., 1968) offers a clear example of an objective value system. Voltaire grew incensed with the capricious actions of the church hierarchy and the French monarchy. To reform the system, he took up his pen and waged a prolific writing campaign. This effort helped humble the church and encouraged the people to topple the monarchy.

We discover Voltaire's value beliefs in his statement, "If a person wishes his country to prosper but never at the expense of other countries, he is at the same time an intelligent patriot and a citizen of the universe."

Objective values are independent of the whims, emotions, and wishes of the individual. The Magna Carta, the U.S. Constitution, and the Napoleonic Code are examples of objective systems. The principles contained in these documents serve as ideal values.

Leaders with objective value systems follow guiding principles that are for the common good. Abraham Lincoln illustrated an objective value system when he said, "A house divided against itself cannot stand." This practical ideal contributed to Lincoln's resolve to resist the separation efforts of the southern states.

Acting to advance the common good is not a selfless process. You benefit from objective standards. So, unless you actively advocate objective principles, you could be at the receiving end of arbitrary practices. Unless you support objective causes, you may find yourself standing alone when you are the target of arbitrary actions. Therefore, when you help protect the liberties of others, you simultaneously protect your rights.

When you operate from objective values, you tend to orient your attention and organize your actions toward *causes:* For example, eliminating starvation or protecting the civil rights of others. Here you use your time and direct your efforts to achieve a "higher purpose."

Let's return to the question: Do you side with your friend or your friend's adversary? If you endorse the views of your friend's opponent, your judgment reflects an objective value system.

Subjective Values

You are a consultant to an automobile company. Management asks you to help them decide an issue about a gasoline tank that may explode in a collision. Your job is to recommend (1) whether the manufacturer should change production methods and move the gasoline tank one foot forward and (2) whether the manufacturer should provide a protective tank shield for earlier-model vehicles without cost to the consumer. You have a computer printout with the following information:

- Retooling and moving the gasoline tank will cost the company $7 million. Shielding the gas tank of older models will cost an additional $8 million. Because of tough competitive conditions, the company can't pass the cost on to the consumer. Therefore, the change could result in lower profits.

- In two years the company will bring out a new design that will end this problem.

- If the model's gasoline tank stays unshielded, there is a 30 percent higher risk that the tank will explode if the automobile gets hit near the tank.

- Risk-management data shows that the exploding tank will not account for more than 15 additional deaths per year for each of the next five years.

- The media probably won't recognize and publicize the defect.

- Actuaries estimate the average loss at $150,000 for each successful lawsuit following a death. The company can settle injuries for an average of $12,000. The insurance companies would pay this cost.

Your advisory fee is 5 percent of the amount of dollars you save the company. If you advise against fixing the problem now, you will net $750,000. If you approve the changes, management will pay you $500.

What would you do? Your response will give you insight into your subjective value system.

Subjective value systems are self-directed, expedient, and oriented toward *interests*. They range from satisfying an urge for ice cream to seeking shelter in a storm. Some subjective values grow out of primitive self-protective drives. We all pursue interests that relate to our survival. However, most of us balance our own interests with a certain cooperation with members of our society to help the group's survival, because we realize joint efforts help us prosper.

Some people operate almost exclusively on subjective values. They have an exploitative "whatever I want I should have" approach to life. Some are tyrants.

Full-fledged tyrants are statistically rare. These are the folk with the capacity to slickly disguise their destructive acts. You normally don't see them unless you have been a target in their destructive games.

Most small-scale tyrants have a craving for power and a need to have public approval. They are inept people who lack the art of leadership and management. They gain authority through ingratiating behavior and by "playing the game." Large-scale tyrants rise on the winds of their manipulative skills. Members of this group can be highly charismatic leaders with the ability to sway crowds.

In response to the gasoline tank issue, if you go for the big money, your decision is subjective.

Humanistic Values

You are driving along a deserted road late on a cold, wet winter night. In your headlight beams, you see a man in ragged clothing. He is shivering. His thumb is up. He holds a half-filled bottle of whiskey. What do you do? The answer to this question may give you insight into your humanistic value system.

Humanistic values involve standards for integrity, trust, and character. You are concerned that others find ways to live dignified and purposeful lives. You actively support their efforts.

Humanistic values guide our people-choices and decisions. A teacher, for example, might discipline you in order to press you to achieve. Another might discipline you out of frustration with your nonsubmissive behavior. You probably can tell the humanist from the egotist.

To return to the hitchhiker question, if you act to shelter the person from the winter cold, you hold humanistic values. Depending upon how you view your personal safety, you might stop your automobile and drive the person to shelter, or you might phone the authorities and have them pick him up for his own safety.

Hedonistic Values

Suppose you could spend a night of pleasure with your fantasy person. After this experience, there is a 50 percent chance you would feel unresponsive toward all future lovers. You have a 10 percent chance of contracting AIDS. What would you do? Your answer to this question can give insight into your hedonistic judgment.

The Greek philosopher Epicurus proclaimed an egotistical hedonism when he said that freedom from pain is the highest good and that people should seek their own pleasure. At the other end of the hedonism spectrum we find the English philosopher David Hume, who defined hedonism as socially approved behavior. Jeremy Bentham went on to say that this utilitarianism is "the greatest good to the greatest number . . . which equals the . . . sum total of human happiness." Psychological hedonism combines Epicurean and Utilitarian ideas. These hedonists seek pleasure that does not cause needless harm to others, preferably in a way that advances the common good.

The psychological hedonist tries to achieve concrete life goals. These goals include the pursuit of wealth, love, health, knowledge, friendship, security, food, and shelter. The psychological hedonist does what feels right because that brings pleasure. This person will act in a self-oriented yet still healthy manner.

Psychological hedonism excludes the pleasures of the happy burglar, the satisfied sadist, and the elated manic. These are pathological patterns that normally don't advance the common good.

Psychological hedonists prefer to experience pleasure and to avoid displeasure. They approach tasks with common sense and act responsibly, because to do otherwise would lead to displeasure and discomfort. Procrastination does not fit this definition of psychological hedonism because procrastination, an act of self-indulgence, leads to tension and grief.

To return to the question that started this section: If you avoid the sexual rendezvous, is it because you do not want to deprive yourself of future sexual delights? If you choose the liaison, is it because you think the meeting is worth the risks? If you consider broader implications — the risks and costs involved if you get infected by the AIDS virus — you are thinking like a psychological hedonist.

Everyday Values

You win a free year-long trip to Tahiti. You would have to quit your job and travel alone. Would you do it? Your answer to that question can give you insight into your everyday value system.

As a practical matter, most people exhibit their objective, subjective, humanistic, and hedonistic values in unique ways. These everyday value directions often consist of more than one value style, and have distinctive features that define one's characteristic way of operating. Once you see how values influence the way people go about their business, you can predict their future actions. Here are some examples that show this everyday value idea:

- Norma, an associate at your office, usually acts responsibly. When she says she'll deliver a report on time, you can take her at her word.

- Tammy Jones bought an economy car. She installed a solar system in her home to save energy, and she circulated a petition in her town for clean air. She fights for animal rights, and she campaigns for liberal political candidates. When she goes to buy a new air conditioner, you know that she's likely to spend a few more dollars for an energy-efficient model.

- Ted Smith bought an inexpensive lawn mower. He brags that he buys no-name brand house paint at closeout prices. Crystal, his wife, says his clothing rack has one suit, which he bought on sale from a discount clothier. When Ted learns he can buy light bulbs for 50 percent off a low discount price, you can be fairly certain he will stock up.

Now let's return to the Tahiti question. Either choice reflects your everyday value system and expresses your basic attitude toward stability.

DEVELOPING AN INTEGRATED VALUE SYSTEM

Without values, your inner world turns like a weather vane in a changing wind—first you go one way and then another, directed exclusively by outside forces. Even subjective values give some direction to life. Think about the value systems we just discussed. What did your choices tell you?

The values you choose represent a choice in direction; they are something that only you can select and develop for yourself. You intentionally develop values through experimentation, reasoning, and reflective thought. If you are not satisfied with or sure of your present values, you can develop higher-order values by doing the following:

- Clarify your values to the point that you understand what your core beliefs are and why you hold them.

- Create opportunities to explore interests outside yourself and to engage in activities that promote the common good.

- Support broader social, economic, or political issues that are important to you.

Contrary to popular belief, we rarely develop these core operating principles by listening to a preacher or reading a book—even this book on change!

Build an Omega Style

Your values serve as a silent compass that gives direction to your life. What direction do you want to take? You can bring together these ideals from objective, hedonistic, and humanistic perspectives, by:

- Acting with fairness and justice
- Enjoying your life
- Contributing your resources to your community

This combination is what I call the omega value style.

This omega value style is different from everyday values because it excludes egotistical subjective values and represents an intentional, active, constructive process of value development.

For omega value development, experiment with potentially enjoyable activities that both absorb your interests and shape your talents. These activities might include appreciating or creating works of art, reading or writing, constructing or restoring, relating, teaching, counseling, or negotiating. Find ways to contribute your gifts; engage in appealing activities where you feel committed. Strive to maintain an objective perspective while still enjoying what you are doing.

As you develop your omega values, you create opportunities for adventure and growth. As with the acquisition of knowledge, there is no endpoint to this process. So shoot for the highest omega level you can attain. You'll have clearer choices and fewer conflicts.

POSTSCRIPT

The evolution of value systems—or decline in values—mirrors the evolution of culture. The more complex our culture, the more we profit from basic values to help guide our decisions.

The differences between how people relate to change partially reflect their values. Some people strive for excellence. Some live by their integrity. Some block the rights of other people. Some value human dignity. Some value animal rights over human life. Through your experiments in testing your guiding principles, you will learn where and when to encourage change in yourself and where to resist changes that violate your values.

The next two chapters will help you see the wide variety of changes that are possible for you, and will help you prepare for the positive change you want to make.

5

The Wheel Is in Your Hands

On a chilly autumn day I watched a flock of graceful Canadian geese take flight. I saw them glide first in one direction, then another. They had a compelling instinct to change location. After finding a bearing, they flew south.

South is the right way to go in the fall of the year, but that is beside the point. At some time in the future, it will be the wrong way to go, but some silly goose will fly there anyway. So much the worse for goosekind! They have no choice but to follow their natural drives.

Unlike geese, who have limited choices, humans can obey, change, direct, or ignore their natural urges. However, with choice comes responsibility, that is, responsibility for taking the steps to effect the choice.

TAKING CONTROL OF YOUR CHOICES

You can change because you have choices. You may not always see them, but they are there. Indeed, despite all our physical and mental frailties, this ability of ours to reason and to alter course is far greater than that of any other creature. That is why we have called ourselves "the knowing animal who knows it is knowing."

As biochemist Albert Szent-Györgyi (1963) explains, the sole purpose of the human brain is to seek advantage. The sheer size of our brains, compared with those of other creatures, affirms that this choice-making is very much what we are about as living creatures. Having the ability to make choices, however, is both a benefit and a burden. The benefit is that we don't have to accept the fate that an indifferent universe hands out. The burden is that by choosing one course, we lose the chance to follow others. So a certain degree of discomfort over lost opportunities is a necessary part of growth.

Learning to bear this discomfort and make choices is a big part of personal development and will help you achieve your change objectives. In order to make the best choices available, you need to open your eyes to the many options you have.

Starting with what I call the "biplane ride," I'll use this chapter to show you techniques for expanding your perception of the range of choices.

The Biplane Ride Technique

Picture yourself flying a biplane. Once you're in the cockpit, you can shift directions at will. You can move the control stick backward and forward and from side to side to make yourself go up, then down, then to the right, and then to the left. Now, just for the fun of it, can you see yourself soaring upward through fluffy clouds before swooping just above the tips of giant trees?

Within limits, you can choose where you want your plane to go. You choose what you want to see. You decide what you want to do. When you choose to steer your plane, you discover your "self."

It doesn't take long to find out that you can steer in some directions but not others. You also find the biplane ride has bumps.

You can't control everything, even on a biplane ride. The currents, for example, lift you through the air. There will always be turbulence to cause the plane to shake, bounce, and go off course. Life is like that too. Still, unexpected destinations may be just what you were looking for without knowing it.

In using the biplane ride technique, you discover that natural impediments will limit you. Some mountains, for instance, will be too tall to fly over. You'll have to fly around them, for to do otherwise could prove to be a fatal mistake. You also learn that responsible restrictions increase your freedom. Thus, a restriction such as a tight seatbelt may feel confining, but it allows you the freedom to turn a barrel roll. Similarly, in your down-to-earth existence, you may choose to study long hours to pass an important exam instead of knocking back a few drinks in front of the tube. You gain an advantage from this act of responsibility.

With all the risks of flying through the sky, you might decide to stay at a low altitude and dally above a familiar field. This may feel safe. If that is what you want, you have the right to make that choice. You have to understand, however, that this safe choice means you will not experience high-speed adventure.

Where would you like to go on your biplane? Perhaps to where you feel real, to new and worthy experiences, to a peaceful inner place. To get there, pick something you'd like to do—an experience that is within your reach. Write it down.

You have to begin somewhere. What you pick is a start. But keep an eraser handy. You may want to change your mind.

The TAG Technique

To change, you will normally have to do something. Whenever you want to go from where you are to somewhere else, you reach your destination by taking some action. This is the idea of the biplane ride—you pick your direction by making choices and following through with your actions. If you want to get to the other side of the street, you walk. If you want to gain self-confidence, you develop your talents. If you want to be a good negotiator, you learn more about negotiating techniques and practice until you master them.

The TAG technique will give you the steps you can take to act on your choices. As shown in the following diagram, first you *T*hink, then *A*ct, to reach your *G*oal!

T ⟶ A ⟶ G

There are different ways to play TAG. Suppose that, as many people do, you get great ideas but let them become overripe and spoil. You can play TAG to determine what you need to do to make the changes that can bring closure to your ideas. For example, the Action might be to take out a patent or a copyright that will give you public ownership of your concept or product (the Thought). If you want to build physical stamina (the Thought), visit health clubs to see which have programs that fit your interests. Sign up and then show up. Take a half-hour walk each night. Walk up stairs rather than take the elevator. Buy an exercise bike, then use it! (Actions)

You can't play TAG without doing something. When you think about change, think about the TAG technique.

THE SIGNIFICANCE OF ACTION

The *A* in TAG is the part of the equation we can see. Is it something you think about trying or something you do? If you want to make an inner change, do you commit yourself to try? What does this mean?

Let's say I asked you to try to blink your eyes rapidly. Go ahead. Blink them. Chances are you can blink your eyes in fast succession. You don't try. You simply do it.

This exercise may look pointless, but it isn't. You can take actions that produce known results. If you say you will try and then do nothing of substance, then saying you'll try may simply be an excuse for doing nothing. "Trying" to do something you *can* do is normally an excuse for inaction!

We often confuse trying with doing. For example, how often have you said, "I'll try to be on time," then arrived late? When you say you will try to be on time, you fool yourself. That is something you do. If you set your goal to save more money each month, don't try to save—just do it! If your goal is to express your feelings, don't try—just do it!

The idea of trying applies to those situations where you don't control the outcome. For example, you try to defeat your opponents in chess or basketball. You don't *try* to play the game, you just do it, even though you can't be certain of the result. Trying also can mean striving for improvement.

Doing gets it done and creates change. Trying shows our willingness to experiment.

The Trim Tab Technique

When a pilot changes the trim tab of an airplane wing or rudder, the craft makes a slight turn in heading. The change is a minor adjustment, and yet it greatly reduces the effort of flying.

A slight change can make a big difference in other ways. For example, a superstar hitter in baseball may bat .350. A very fine hitter may bat .300. The difference? The .350 hitter gets seven hits each 20 times at bat. The .300 hitter gets six. In the same spirit, a gradual shift in outlook can transform dormant energy into accomplishment. This minor adjustment is the trim tab effect.

You can make a slight shift in one part of your life that will make a big difference in all the other parts. I will show you that you have more choices than you may have thought. Here are some simple examples:

- If you want to lose weight, and spread extra butter on your bread, start by substituting a less-fattening spread such as apple butter.

- If you normally don't greet people at your place of work, start the day by saying hello to your co-workers. Make it a point to greet at least five people before you reach your desk. Your co-workers may start to view you in a new light.

- Show yourself that you can develop quality ideas. Keep a notebook by your desk and jot down one of your ideas by noon each day. On days when you feel discouraged because you lack confidence in your abilities, refer to the notebook. Better yet, test out some of your ideas and see what you can discover.

- If you want to get ahead in your career, try coming to work 15 minutes early and leaving 15 minutes later than usual. Over time you'll get more done than the average person, and you will open opportunities for advancement.

The key to the trim tab technique is to make a small change in your habitual actions. Many small trim tab changes may not seem revolutionary, yet the long-term effects may be dramatic. Why? The cumulative effects of even minor adjustments are often much greater than a revolutionary one-shot action.

The Discovery Technique

Fortunate events, coordinated plans, paradoxes, insights, rational thinking, fantasies, myths, risks, experimentation, and *choice*—all stimulate discovery, which in turn stimulates change.

Discovery learning is learning by accident, but the person who sees the opportunity in the accident gains the advantage. To learn through discovery, you have to involve yourself in conditions that shift the odds in your favor.

Eminent Russian physiologist Ivan Pavlov began an investigation into the salivary responses in dogs. He observed that when a trainer approached the dog with food, the dog started to salivate. The dog's anticipatory response caused difficulties in measuring what was supposed to be the main focus of the study. Pavlov's assistants wanted to control the dog's preliminary reaction or get rid of it. Pavlov decided to study it instead. His investigation of behavior that he had discovered by accident led to the formulation of the now-famous conditioned reflex theory.

We can create the opportunities for discovery, almost at will. For example, when we make assumptions before examining the facts, we risk drawing false conclusions. Intentionally testing one's assumptions, however, can lead to discovery.

To use the discovery technique, consciously put yourself in someone else's shoes. Seeing a problem from another's perspective can open up a whole new range of choices. If you are a manager, for example, try doing the work of some of your subordinates. You may discover procedures that will save costs, improve quality, or reduce fatigue.

The message is clear. If you stretch your resources, you follow a path of discovery. But you won't know for sure what is on that path until you walk along it.

THE LESSONS OF DOUBLE TROUBLE

The phenomenon of double trouble sometimes makes us feel that our choices are limited. "Double trouble" happens when two unfortunate events occur in sequence. The first trouble is a basic response to an unpleasant or undesirable condition. For example, you are frustrated and disappointed over the impending loss of your job. You create the second trouble when you layer an unnecessary problem onto a frustration and then laminate them: You make yourself anxious by telling yourself you can't cope with the job loss.

You get yourself into more double trouble when you make yourself anxious over your anxiety by telling yourself that you should not feel anxious and must act calm. Now you have doused the original frustration with misery and anguish. You would have been better off riding out the original turbulence.

Double trouble is like the pink elephant dilemma. The more you blame yourself for having a problem, the worse you feel. Let's see how this works. Don't think of a pink elephant for the next 30 seconds. What happens? Do you think of a pink elephant? Do you try to imagine a blue fox instead? I'll bet that the harder you concentrate on forgetting the pink elephant (or the blue fox), the more compelling the image becomes.

There is a way out of the pink elephant trap. If you accept the pink elephant image and don't feel compelled to erase it from your mind, it will vaporize soon enough. If you accept your frustration for what it is—frustration and nothing more—you'll avoid double-trouble thinking and the accompanying exaggerated tension that accompanies this process.

The pink elephant helps us understand a critical change lesson. People who accept their unwanted feelings are less burdened by them than those who strain to squelch these feelings. For example, consider the common situation of an individual (Tony) who plans to give a speech before his Rotary Club with the intention of making a sterling impression and improving his image with the group.

Tony worries about his performance. He anguishes over forgetting his lines, showing cracks in his voice, clearing his throat, and stumbling over his words. He draws a picture in his mind of a comic character who gets laughed out of the Rotary. This performance anxiety is enough of a problem. Yet there is more. He knows he is exaggerating his problem and lowering his chances for a quality performance. So he blames himself for this anticipatory anxiety. He bears down on himself with demands that he stop feeling anxious. He tells himself, "Stop doing this to yourself!" He tortures himself this way because he thinks he can't stand feeling nervous and must grasp for some resolution; perhaps a commandment to stop will do the trick. Unfortunately, his commands escalate his problem to heights of sheer misery. In this pressured effort, he symbolically throws psychological gasoline on already hot emotional flames.

Tony believes that he should totally control himself, and this belief is the major source of his distress. He has created his own living nightmare.

Tony changes when he figures out there is no universal dictate that people should always — or even frequently — have total control over their thoughts and feelings. It helps him to know that Sir Laurence Olivier suffered from stage fright his whole life. If Olivier lived through his anxiety, Tony reasons, he can live through his.

As he begins to accept that feeling uncomfortable in a new situation is normal, Tony feels less anticipatory anxiety. He realizes that people can feel uncomfortable because of psychological processes they don't understand or because they lack information. Also, some situations are just very uncomfortable! As Tony gathers information about this process, he feels more comfortable with himself and with his life because he understands that he does not have to feel comfortable to do a good job at public speaking. He wisely concentrates on his audience and what he is saying rather than on how well he is doing and how comfortable he is feeling. He learns that although he is unable to control his natural discomfort, he can choose to avoid overreacting.

I see many people like Tony who try too hard to control tense feelings, only to make themselves feel worse. They get into double trouble when they find they can't force a negative emotion out of existence. I see this in clients who preoccupy themselves with their worries and troubles so much that they have trouble falling asleep. If you think you need to get a good night's sleep and then tell yourself, "I've got to fall asleep, I've got to fall asleep!" you might get angry with yourself for staying awake and lessen your chances for falling asleep.

Who could easily fall asleep under such self-badgering conditions? The solution? Recognize that even if you worry about staying awake, you will get rest if you lie still. You probably will slip into and out of sleep and get more rest than you think.

The Quartz Stone Technique

You can use your imagination and this simple technique to rid yourself of double trouble. Find a small quartz stone. First, hold it tight. Then hold it gently. As you let go of the tension, imagine your double trouble flowing into the stone. Pretend the stone is like a diode where current flows only one way. Thus, the troubles flowing from your hand stay trapped in the stone. When you have imagined that enough negative energy has flowed into the stone, throw it away. The quartz stone technique can help remind you that by letting go of the need for control, you can achieve a relaxed state of mind.

Shakespeare said, "There is nothing either good or bad but thinking makes it so." Whether you relive, in vivid color, a particularly unpleasant experience or anticipate, with equal gore, a future one, the problem is often due more to your thoughts about the experience than to the experience itself.

This oscillation between remembrance and anticipation detracts from the present moment. The secret, then, is to deal with right now right now. Right now there is no guilt, for guilt reflects the past. Right now there is no frightful event, for anxiety is about the future. If you can't think of anything else to think about, just look at the back of your hand. What you see is what is happening right now. Not too scary, is it?

Psychiatrist Abraham Low (1950) gives us another perspective on this double-trouble problem of fearing to face discomfort. He rightly points out that the more you anticipate the discomfort, the greater the fear you will feel. Instead of thinking "I cannot stand discomfort," you are wise to redefine the problem as "I care not to stand the discomfort." You can't change a "cannot," but you can change a "care not." Now, how can you bring yourself to tolerate something you don't like?

THE MYTH OF THE MAGIC CRYSTALS

Early one spring morning, as the friendly rays of the sun streamed through the trees on the Argon Mountains, Carol arrived at the cave of Delphi, a mysterious wolf-human with the power to foresee the future.

Carol cautiously approached the cave and knocked on the massive oak door. Slowly it opened. Once she was inside, the door slammed shut behind her.

Carol found herself in a world illuminated by the sparkling light of pine torches. The glow from the flames sent shadows dancing everywhere.

She wondered where Delphi was, but before she could raise her voice to speak, the prophet appeared before her.

"What do you wish to know?" Delphi asked softly.

Carol knew this strong wolf-beast could devour her in a moment. Yet Delphi sounded compassionate and gentle.

Carol told Delphi that she was a good mother who worked hard so her family would never know hunger. She supported her husband's wishes and helped her family and friends.

She believed her life had passed her by. Now in her middle years, she wanted her just reward. She wanted to relive her life. With that she said, "I want my youth returned. I want my body transformed back into the svelte body of a young woman. I will pay a bag of gold if you make my body as firm and my skin as soft as it was when I was eighteen. Please, I ask only for what is fair." Delphi disappeared, then returned with two glimmering crystal globes. Suddenly the crystal in the beast's right paw began to shimmer with eerie red and blue light. Within the sphere, Carol saw an unearthly hologram of herself, an image of how she might look in ten years—older, downtrodden, out-of-shape. Then the other crystal flamed into yellow light. Carol saw herself as older, but thinner, firmer, and attractive, and at peace with herself.

Amazed at the power of the crystal globes, she could hardly

contain herself. "Yes!" Carol said in a tone of pure excitement. "The one on your left. That is how I want to be!"

The wolf-human responded by blowing softly on the incandescent crystals. Right before Carol's eyes, the firm image weakened and the humbled image grew until they converged to reflect how she looked that day. Then the red and blue and yellow radiance faded, flickered, and died.

Delphi said, "I cannot turn back time. You must take the future for what it is. Go back to your world and remember that past deeds are but food for memories."

Stunned by the experience, Carol left the cave with two thoughts. "Others cannot transform me by magic; I am the only one who can change me. I cannot go back to the past, but I can shape my physical form and create an inner world where I am at peace with myself."

Delphi bestowed a valuable gift by showing Carol that she had choices. Still, it takes more than an initial insight to change. Carol had to take charge of herself and shape her future. There are hard choices to make. We often have to give something up to gain something else. Sometimes we give up a set of worn-out assumptions to gain ground.

How to Use the Myth

You can plug habits and patterns into the two imaginary crystals and predict what happens if you go one way or another. If you have a drinking problem, picture yourself continuing to consume alcohol, and imagine how you will change over the years. This is not a pretty picture, and I'll say no more about what happens when you choose to have no choice. Then imagine yourself sober. You'll have many joys and many sorrows, good times and painful times. The road will be rough. Yet, you will steer your life. If you procrastinate, imagine putting procrastination in one crystal ball. Visualize this faithless companion leading you along paths of stress and strain with limited gains. Remove procrastination from the picture and you have many accomplishments and a firmer sense of self. You choose the way you want to develop and you will know your future.

Most of our self-defeating habits are changeable. They are merely behaviors that we decide not to control! By breaking these habits, we can face a new direction and choose change over stagnation.

POSTSCRIPT

You hold the wheel. You decide where you want to go, and you choose the resources needed to get there. Like the work of the pilot, your perceptions and memories of changing landmarks will differ from those of the passengers'. Passengers may get lost if they later travel the road alone. The pilot discovers the way and remembers the direction.

You can change more than any other creature because you can think, make choices, and carry out thoughtful action. To change, all you need to do is command your body to move and your mind to see from different angles.

6

Change and Rational Thinking

W e've come a long way since Ferdinand Magellan's voyages proved that the world was round. Since then our fears of falling off the edge of the earth have vanished, but other erroneous beliefs have replaced them.

Face it, we all harbor some erroneous beliefs that can blur our perceptions and block change. The trick is to detect them and strip them of their power. In Chapter 2 we discussed building a rational perspective. In this chapter I'll show you how to harness that rational perspective and use it to achieve the change you want.

USING YOUR RATIONAL PERSPECTIVE

Can you think your way into good mental health by stripping yourself of misconceptions and other mental pitfalls? Rational-emotive behavior therapy (REBT) says that you can.

Albert Ellis, the noted psychologist who developed REBT, built his system on an idea similar to one that William James (1892), the founder of American psychology, found so valuable. To

James, the most important discovery of the twentieth century was that people could change their lives by changing their thinking.

REBT was developed around four main ideas: (1) we feel the way we think, (2) we largely create our own emotional disturbances, (3) we can learn to undisturb ourselves, and (4) we can apply rational principles to solve problems and to be happier.

Ellis (1990) uses a simple ABC model to chart the path to change. He links *A*ctivating events, *B*eliefs about those events, and *C*onsequences.

Your beliefs are at the center of the ABC system. For example: Suppose you are on your way to a job interview. You took special care to dress attractively and project an upbeat appearance. As you walk to the interview site, a truck swerves to your side of the street and hits a puddle. A miniature tidal wave drenches you from head to toe. Startled, you jump to a conclusion: "The driver did it on purpose and deserves to hang!" If you had this idea, how would you feel?

Most people with that thought would feel anger—perhaps rage. Now let's add information you would not have had before. You now see a small child running frightened from the middle of the street. You conclude that the driver swerved to miss the child. Would you feel differently about the event? If so, you have changed your belief, and you may not see the truck driver the same way as you did before.

There comes a time where we question why some people are affected differently by similar events. Not everyone, for example, would have the same reaction to the splashing incident. The answer partially lies with the person's perceptions of the situation. For example: Consider two war veterans who were in the same unit and lived through the same battles. One feels afraid whenever he hears a helicopter motor near a wooded area; to him, the helicopter symbolizes his fear of death. The other feels an unusual sense of relief; the helicopter symbolizes a return from the battlefield and safety. Without their war experience, the helicopter would normally have no strong emotional value. So the event promotes memories of itself through symbols of the experience. But it is the person's perceptions, definitions, and conditioned thinking and feeling about a past, present, or anticipated event that determines the direction of that person's emotional response.

Rational and Irrational Thinking

The rational-emotive model categorizes beliefs as either rational or irrational. (Of course, there are other beliefs—religious, political, family, and social—that represent different ideologies which may or may not fit snugly into either rational or irrational categories.) Rational beliefs are reasonable, responsible, objective, flexible, and constructive. When your beliefs are rational, you normally have the perspective, confidence, and tolerance to achieve constructive goals for survival, love, achievement, health, or friendship.

Irrational beliefs do not necessarily cause harmful results. Believing in leprechauns who play tricks on people, for example, would normally fall into this *harmless* category. *Harmful* irrational beliefs, on the other hand, are arbitrary and illusory; they interfere with obtaining constructive goals. Irrational beliefs stem from faulty reasoning that includes misconceptions, overgeneralizations, intolerant demands (neurotic claims that events should, ought to, or must go your way), and other fictions that lead to one or more of these nonproductive results: emotional disturbance, biased judgment, and inappropriate behavior such as avoidance of opportunity, compulsions, or drinking to get drunk.

Irrational beliefs lack validity, which means they can be changed. For example, the belief "I only can feel worthwhile when people approve of me" is invalid, irrational, and harmful. As most of us do, you probably prefer approval to disapproval. However, you needlessly upset yourself when you think you *must* have approval to feel worthwhile.

How can you separate a harmful irrational belief from a rational one when the irrational belief sounds seductively reasonable? You look at the results. Your rational beliefs will prompt actions that lead to accomplishment, happiness, health, or psychological growth. Irrational beliefs interfere with achieving these constructive goals and evoke patterns of nonproductive states such as anxiety, depression, hostility, procrastination, psychopathy, "workaholism," withdrawal, or escapism.

Although distinctions are not as clearcut as we might wish, we can discriminate between rational and harmful irrational beliefs. However, to make this distinction, you would wisely take conditions into account; that is, factor in the environmental context of your belief. For example, a political hostage may believe her guards will protect her from harm. From one vantage point, this is irrational because the guards may have orders to do otherwise once she is no longer useful. On the other hand, the hostage's belief might generate an attitude of friendliness, which could lead to her survival. In that context, the belief is irrational but functional.

Irrational beliefs feel natural when they are well-practiced. Many of the self-defeating thoughts we have today are thoughts we had before—perhaps thousands of times. These are mental rules that produce predictably poor outcomes. They are change-resistive, partially because they are so well-practiced that we act them out without much forethought. Once you see them, you can posture yourself to break these patterns by undermining their rigid authority.

To rid yourself of harmful irrational beliefs, Ellis (1988) advocates Disputing these beliefs and supplanting them with rational beliefs that promote rational Effects. To carry out the D part of his system, Ellis uses Socratic methods, scientific thinking, emotive strategies, and behavior activities. Let's look at some common beliefs I call "hang-up traps" to see how we can recognize and dispute irrational beliefs.

BEATING THE HANG-UP TRAPS

We have strong reactions to many different types of events, such as getting fired from a job, having an unpleasant dream, obsessing over certain events, suffering through a shattered romance, or seeing someone else take credit for our work. If you feel uncomfortable and uncertain about what to do or if you feel unable to cope, you might fall into one or more of the A, B, or C traps. Look closely and you will be able to see the camouflaged beliefs that bait each trap.

The A Trap: Placing Blame

A trap people blame events, because they assume that outside conditions automatically cause distress. Although overcoming noxious conditions has advantages, A trappers seem to believe that the only way to be rid of stressful feelings is to change the event. If they can't change events to their advantage, they feel they have no choice but to suffer.

Activating events, such as the loss of a limb, can jar your inner world. Still, railing at an unfortunate event is as ineffective as anguishing over anguish. Thus, when you routinely blame people or conditions for how you feel, you miss these important pieces to the change puzzle: (1) You are the author of your thoughts and emotions; (2) the event is the stage, but you are the director; (3) sometimes unpleasant happenings occur on this stage, but you have control over your thinking about the event; and (4) clear thinking will get you farther than will blaming the circumstances.

You change *A* trap patterns when you take responsibility for your feelings and actions without condemning yourself or anyone else. Suppose you have a roommate who messes up your living area with dirty dishes, old newspapers, and smelly socks. You feel angry because you believe your sloppy roommate *must* change for you to feel comfortable. You try to change this person with threats. Now you have two problems: sloppiness and conflict. Now, suppose the good clothing fairy left $1,000 under your pillow each time your roommate acted sloppily. I'll bet the money would add variety to your beliefs about the meaning of a pair of old socks on the floor.

Once you accept that you author your feelings, you will probably still dislike your roommate's messiness. But now you can face the issue and in a noncondemning tone, try to persuade your roommate to change. You could also find a new roommate.

Although events can forcefully attract attention, your *interpretation* of the event strongly influences how you feel and what you do. You have four reasonable choices: (1) Change unwanted conditions, (2) reframe your thinking, (3) reframe your thinking *and* change unwanted conditions, or (4) accept the situation without caterwauling.

The *B* Trap: Analysis Paralysis

The Dutch Philosopher Benedict Spinoza tells us that emotions are a frequent link between associated ideas. For example, the thought of one injustice links to another injustice, and before long you have a list of past grievances angrily buzzing through your mind. These thoughts and feelings are painfully stifling. To escape this snare, *B* trap people work to make airtight cases to justify the nobility of their cause and to overcome the emotional entanglements they create for themselves. Paradoxically, instead of making life better, they work themselves deeper into a mental prison of their own making.

B trap people grab for control when they use their intellect to try to squelch the emotional responses that flow from the very irrational beliefs they want to justify. By trying too hard to have control, they overwhelm themselves with tension. Their primary tool to gain control is analysis, and they often suffer from what I call "analysis paralysis."

Analysis paralysis occurs when *B* trap people break their personal problems down to minute details so they can figure out why they—and others—feel and act as they do. They double-check their thinking to make sure they have the right beliefs, right information, right everything. They engage in this microanalysis to remove uncertainty and to guarantee they can control uncomfortable thoughts, feelings, and behaviors. Invariably the plan backfires because they are so busy analyzing that they don't act to change!

Some *B* trappers also make irrational "should," "ought to," "must" demands. For example, the *B*-trapped person who forgets a line of a speech concludes, "I *should* never have made a mistake in public!" The message is that *what is, should not have been.* Such irrational demands are impossible to meet because you can't change the past!

If you find that you are in the *B* trap, you have many points of exit. Focus on a desired accomplishment that is within your reach. Then act! Recognize where and why you are indecisive. Rather than going around and around in your thoughts, seek clarity through testing some of your beliefs against reality. Know that you can spring the trap and knock out irrational beliefs with facts that come from reality checking.

The *C* Trap: Needless Worry

There are two versions of the *C* trap: emotions and response. You fall into one trap when you worry too much about how you feel and into the other when you get hung up about your actions or habits.

Emotions. People who fall into the emotional consequences (EC) trap preoccupy themselves with their feelings. They want to stop feeling depressed. They lament about the length of time they have felt stressed—as though there was a time limit. This is like being in a storm and insisting that the winds stop blowing *now!*

You fall into the EC trap because you want complete control over your emotions. So you carefully monitor your emotional thermometer. When you feel *good*, you still worry whether the feeling will last, and you therefore lose the feeling because of the *worry.*

An emotional goal of feeling good misses the point. Feeling good is a byproduct of what you think and do and of outer conditions, which you often help create, that stimulate these feelings. You can escape the EC trap by accepting your feelings and using your stress emotions as signals to help you get to the root of your problems.

Response. People who fall into the response consequences (RC) trap have self-defeating habits which they blame for their problems. If only they could stop binging, they'd lose weight. If only they could act with cordial grace, they would get better job opportunities. If only they could stop bickering, they could have meaningful relationships. The "if only" list goes on and on. This group is distinguished by placing symbol over substance: "Did I sound right?" "Did I look okay?" For them, life is a rehearsed speech!

You can break this trap by asking yourself problem-solving questions and then acting on your rational answers. These questions include: What did I tell myself to stimulate my actions? How did I feel? What thoughts and feelings connect with my habit pattern? What is my path for change? You also can use the stepping out of character technique from Chapter 2 to act effectively, and thus avoid the *C* trap.

The *A, B,* and *C* traps often flow together. An emotional consequence of an irrational belief can stimulate you to think about how you feel, and these thoughts can lead to greater emotional agitation and lapses in performance. These conditions, in turn, lead to more analysis paralysis, anxiety over your inaction, and the feeling you are in a hopeless rut. Use problem solving and break this cycle of thought.

You can also use the following rational strategies to fuel your constructive change efforts and stay out of the *A, B,* and *C* traps.

CHANGING IRRATIONAL BELIEFS

When you find yourself "locked in" by irrational thoughts, disturbed feelings, and self-defeating actions, use the *stop, listen,* and *act* method. Use it whenever you put yourself down or feel depressed, anxious, or angry. It goes like this:

1. Stop. Put your thoughts into slow motion.

2. Listen to what you are telling yourself.

3. Act to identify, clarify, and dispute irrational beliefs using one or more of the following five rational-emotive strategies.

The Reality Confrontation Strategy

Reality is sometimes an effective teacher that causes you to make rapid changes. For example, a client told me that while riding his bicycle he believed he would have an accident unless he closed his eyes. He shut his eyes, bounced against a wall, and landed in a trash can. After that, he kept his eyes wide open while bicycling.

We learn fast when we believe our life is in immediate peril. But when future projections are not so immediate, we may not act to change deadly patterns. How many smokers know that they risk cancer and heart disorders, yet continue to smoke? Despite compelling evidence that they can die a painful death, how many kick the habit? How about people on high-fat diets who refuse to change their eating patterns? For them, anticipation does not teach.

Reality is a slow teacher in other ways. A client I'll call Margaret, who had married and divorced four men, wanted to know why she had problems maintaining these relationships. Our discussions revealed that each of her husbands had reminded her of her father, whom she remembered as a reclusive, withdrawn, emotionally constipated man. Margaret believed she could transform these husbands into sensitive, loving, caring people.

Each time, the plan didn't work. I was able to show her that her four marriages followed the same pattern. She went for men who gave her a feeling of familiarity. She used the wrong selection criteria. If you want a warm, loving mate, you need to find someone who is warm and loving *before* you get married.

By looking at her selection criteria, and the results of her marriages, she quickly saw how she could avoid repeating the mistake. Her key to change lay in using a two-step reality confrontation strategy that allowed her to understand her behavior and change it. You can also employ this strategy.

1. Find common threads. In our temporal and spatial world, one moment blends into the next in a constant flow. Yet we can make the content of our thoughts a stop-and-go affair. Margaret learned to suspend these past events in her mind and pause to see the significance of the common threads that wove through her relationship with her father and her four ex-husbands.

2. Apply new interpretations to events and experiences. With certain moments in suspended thought, where we hold in our mind a picture of past events, we can analyze them anew and formulate healthy, rational ideas about them. The events remain the same, of course, but we have a fresh, helpful view of reality. Margaret used this strategy to reassess her relationship with her father.

Through this exercise, she learned that she did not need to debase her human worth because her father was unloving. That was *his* problem. She could still accept herself without his love and approval. She did not need to run a reform school for husbands to relive and resolve her childhood conflicts.

The Coping Statements Strategy

You can use rational coping statements to counter irrational beliefs that have soaked your mind and dampened your spirits. Let's look at some common self-defeating beliefs and the coping statements you can use to disrupt each one.

To use this coping method effectively, make sure the coping statement is meaningful, phrase it in objective terms, and present the statement to yourself in an assertive tone.

Self-Defeating Beliefs	**Rational Coping Statements**
People should always treat me fairly.	I don't like it when I am not treated fairly, but I realize the world is not always as fair as I would like it to be.
I can't stand it when things don't go my way.	I can stand what I don't like. I can work to accept what I don't like but can't change. I can change that which is changeable.
I should be able to do whatever I want whenever I want.	Limitations in life are inevitable. Freedom comes from restricting my choices to activities that constructively improve the quality of my life.
Other people make me feel and act the way I do.	I am the one who makes me feel and act as I do.

Coping statements have limitations. Parroting statements without connecting them to a believable reality normally won't work. Also, fluffy statements such as, "I am getting better every day in every way" do little. What if you are doing worse? Similarly, if you feel depressed and try to tell yourself you feel happy, the statement strategy won't work. You can, however, strengthen the effectiveness of your coping statements by following these simple procedures:

- Make a written description of an event that evoked a specific stressful emotion, such as anxiety.

- Write your major anxious thought about the event, such as "I can't cope."

- Create a brief, clear, meaningful, and rational self-assertion to counter the thought, such as "I don't like this situation but I can deal with it rationally."

- Next time you feel anxious, match your coping statements against your anxious thoughts.

Now, how can you verify if your coping statements are rational? If you can answer yes to two or more of the five following questions, chances are the statement is rational:

- Does your statement point to constructive changes?

- Is the statement valid?

- Does the idea enhance your relationships with other people?

- Does your statement encourage tolerance and self-acceptance?

- Does your statement sound sensible and reasonable?

A coping statement becomes a belief when you trust the idea and feel an emotional commitment to it. For this to happen, the idea would best have relevance, rationality, and a close tie to experience.

The Disputing Faulty Belief Systems Strategy

Disputing irrational belief systems involves a very advanced type of thinking: falsifying beliefs through disconfirmation. Pat's case shows how she successfully falsified a set of irrational beliefs.

Pat returned to school to complete her degree in education. After the first semester she convinced herself she was worthless because she had a difficult time mastering educational statistics. She received an average grade for the course. This was a very serious problem for her, because the average grade symbolized failure and failure signified worthlessness.

- The activating event was an average grade in statistics.

- Her disturbing irrational belief was: "I am a stupid worthless person for getting an average grade. I should not be in school."

- Her emotional consequences were feelings of worthlessness and depression.

She set as her goal acceptance of herself even if she failed all of her courses. Here are the questions she used and her rational answers:

- How does an average grade in statistics make me an inferior being? *Rational answer:* The course proved more time-consuming and the subject more difficult to master than I had originally thought. The resulting grade has nothing to do with my inner worth but does reflect the teacher's estimation of my skill level in this course. A school grade is different from a self-worth report card, which is never final.

- Do I apply the same perfectionist standards to others, or am I uniquely critical toward myself? *Rational answer:* I know of other students who have received average grades or lower. I think well of them for trying. I do not have to be so hard on myself.

- If I had failed statistics, how would that make me worthless? *Rational answer:* A failing grade does not mark me as an inferior person. My humanity goes beyond definition. So I'd wisely accept that statistics is not my strongest subject, but I would still wisely do the very best I can.

As an outcome of this exercise, Pat reinforced her rational beliefs: "It's too bad I did not get a higher grade. I would prefer to have done better. My human worth, however, is different from a grade!" With that, she felt less stressed.

To apply the disputing faulty belief systems strategy, ask yourself these five questions:

1. What do I believe about this situation?

2. What beliefs can I verify?

3. What is the most plausible conclusion I can draw from the facts I have?

4. What additional information would let me make a reliable inference?

5. What is my most responsible course of action? (What is my behavior response?)

The Activity Assignment Strategy

Activity assignments involve testing new ways of thinking, feeling, and acting. Clara's case illustrates a rational activity assignment.

This bright, critical person regarded imperfect people as blameworthy and punishable for their faults. She fantasized about flogging people who showed flaws in their abilities. When I met her, she felt lonely, distressed, worn out, and unhappy about her life.

I gave Clara four activity assignments to help her overcome her critical outlook. The goal was for her to build tolerance.

First, I asked her to describe, in writing, her aptitudes and skills. Then she ranked them from strongest to weakest. Next she asked herself if her weaker skills characterized her worth. She got the picture from this exercise and saw that she had strengths and weaknesses that varied from situation to situation. These variances had nothing to do with her worth, but did reflect changing skills in changing circumstances.

In the second week I asked her to observe the strengths and weaknesses of three of her co-workers and to note how their qualities varied by situation. She found that her co-workers complemented each other's strengths, and each showed variances in their performances.

During the third week she spent 30 minutes a day using her critical thinking skill to disconfirm her original belief that "mistake makers" are failures. As a result, she reported feeling more tolerant toward error.

At week four I asked her to work at accepting other people's errors without condemning them. What could she learn from their mistakes? This exercise helped her to think more flexibly and tolerantly about human fallibility.

As a byproduct of this experiment, Clara started to empathize with people and tolerate their mistakes. Her veil of depression lifted. She made a few good friends.

The activity assignment strategy can be very effective if you follow these six guidelines:

1. Identify and clarify your problem.

2. Define attainable, measurable goals.

3. Design experiments to test rational ways of thinking, feeling, and acting.

4. Act out the change.

5. Measure the results.

6. Use feedback to support or revise the plan.

The Rational-Emotive Imagery Strategy

If you can create anxiety-provoking images, you also can create images to defuse anxiety. That is the idea behind rational-emotive imagery.

You can use rational-emotive imagery (REI) to see how your thinking influences how you feel and how your feelings influence your thinking. For example: Try to re-create your feelings during a stressful event. Experience the anxiety. Make yourself feel as tense as you can. Now change the feeling to concern. When you change the feeling, do you hear a different story in your mind?

Let's try another example. Imagine an experience when you felt humiliated or embarrassed. Revive the situation from your memory. Get into the feeling. Now what are you thinking? I'll bet it is, "I feel so exposed. They see my weakness. How awful." Now make yourself feel regretful. Hold the feeling. Concentrate on that emotion. Now what are you thinking? If you feel regret, you will likely think something like, "Too bad. I wish I had not exposed a fault. How unfortunate."

You can change irrational ideas by changing your emotions. Be aware, however, that not all emotional responses could or should be altered. For example, being saddened by the loss of a friend is appropriate and valid, although you don't feel "good" with that response. No rational belief need be changed. The purpose of the REI strategy is to let you accept natural feelings such as sadness, desire, or frustration without squelching them and to change discretionary emotions such as anxiety into feelings that are appropriate for the situation.

Using REI effectively is not necessarily the linear and automatic process that it first appears to be. Temporary changes in feelings will not necessarily become permanent changes. You may not have complete control over the change of feelings, but you can do much to reduce needless distress founded on irrational assumptions.

TESTING YOUR PROGRESS

You now have several strategies for challenging harmful irrational beliefs.

After you apply the five strategies, use the following questions and rating scale to gauge your progress. Keep track of your responses to see how they change over time.

1. Do you feel you have more self-control?

Frequently 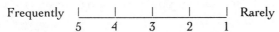 Rarely

               5   4   3   2   1

2. Do you feel more intensely about matters you value?

Frequently |_____|_____|_____|_____|_____| Rarely

               5   4   3   2   1

3. Do you experience less stress?

Frequently |_____|_____|_____|_____|_____| Rarely

               5   4   3   2   1

4. Do you find you are less judgmental?

Frequently |_____|_____|_____|_____|_____| Rarely

               5   4   3   2   1

5. Are you willing to test new ideas?

Frequently |_____|_____|_____|_____|_____| Rarely

               5   4   3   2   1

6. Are you thinking more self-accepting thoughts?

Frequently |_____|_____|_____|_____|_____| Rarely

               5   4   3   2   1

7. Are you thinking more thoughts that demonstrate self-efficacy?

Frequently |_____|_____|_____|_____|_____| Rarely

               5   4   3   2   1

8. Are you acting to produce the results you seek?

Frequently 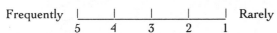 Rarely

               5   4   3   2   1

Your response numbers should go up as you use your rational perspective to create the change you want.

POSTSCRIPT

Rational-emotive thinking gives you at least five cognitive, emotive, and behavior directions for change:

- By changing false beliefs, you can change associated feelings and problem habits.

- By changing your problem habits, you change associated beliefs and feelings.

- By eliminating emotional distress, you change associated beliefs and problem habits.

- By altering negative circumstances, you reduce the incidence of unwanted activating events.

- By making constructive changes, you develop self-efficacy and strengthen your core self.

Let's move on to Part Two of this book, where we'll put your newly developed sense of self to work for change.

Part Two

Moving Forward
The Master Plan

7

Your Five-Point Change Program

I n this part of your journey, you will learn a five-point change program that describes how you can change and keep moving forward. The program is like a map. To learn a new territory you must travel through it, and the map helps to guide you to any of a number of destinations you choose. The techniques and strategies you acquired in Part One will help you to master the five-point program and achieve the change you want.

This Five-Point Change Program is different from the five stages of change we discussed in Chapter 1. The five stages tell you *what happens as you change.* The Five-Point Change Program tells you *what you can do to change.* You can apply this five-point "hands-on" action method to practically any significant challenge in your life, including many not covered in this book.

Your Five-Point Change Program is the first component of your 5–1–5 change system. The program is applied to *one* life area (or challenge) that you want to change (or meet), where you proceed through *five* stages of change as you achieve mastery over that area. This concentration on critical challenges can have sweeping benefits. What you do today to improve the quality of one significant aspect of your life can ripple through other areas, helping you meet other critical challenges. The procrastinator who learns to act responsibly will get more done and thus experience less stress. The person hooked on problem habits who adopts healthier behavior patterns will discover a more positive self-concept.

In this chapter, you will learn how to use the Five-Point Change Program. Then in future chapters I will describe how you can apply the system to four critical life areas: building emotional muscle, developing stress tolerance, keeping other people's agendas in perspective, and finding higher levels of career satisfaction.

THE CHANGE GENIE

Remember Aladdin's lamp? Let's pretend for a moment that you find it and rub it. Suddenly a magnificent genie, garbed in richly-colored burgundy silk robes, appears out of a billow of blue smoke. The genie feels most grateful to you for waking him from his slumbers, and says he will grant you one of 15 opportunities. Then he waves his hands and a block of rose-colored marble appears with the names of 15 results carved on its glistening surface. You can pick one of them. You are awestruck as you look at the selection:

1. To manage change wisely

2. To control time

3. To accept yourself

4. To be tolerant

5. To be flexible

6. To be articulate

7. To think reflectively

8. To feel good

9. To act bravely

10. To live with a positive outlook

11. To find satisfaction in your career

12. To enjoy excellent health

13. To live a long life

14. To look young

15. To find exciting sexual partners

"Imagine what I could do if I selected number 2 and could control time," you exclaim. "I could put life into slow motion or speed ahead in time at will. Such power!"

"That is not what I had in mind," the genie says, to your surprise. "The 15 choices are about *you*. You can't control someone else's clock. You can choose only what you will do with your time."

You overcome your triskaidekaphobia and select number 13—to live a long life. Then the genie stumps you by saying, "Yes, you can enjoy a long life, but you are the one to decide what you can do to increase the odds of living a long life."

"Unfair," you howl. "That is not the way it goes in fairy tales."

"Life is not a fairy tale," the genie replies. "You must do something to make the wish come true."

"Well," you snap, "how can I make sure I have a long life?"

The genie's answer is disarmingly simple. "Your wish becomes attainable when you choose the correct actions. For example, you can follow a sound nutritional and exercise program and keep your weight down. You can stay informed about your health status through regular medical examinations. You can promptly deal with stresses of life before they rise to dominate your mind. The goal of attaining a long life is yours to claim. Naturally, your genetics will eventually prevail, but you can do much to add quality to your life and, perhaps, lengthen it."

So you learn that you are your own genie. All 15 choices are yours for the asking. How do you claim them? You can start by following the Five-Point Change Program.

YOUR FIVE-POINT CHANGE PROGRAM

You can't have full control over a changing world because you cannot know or manipulate all events. Nevertheless, you can give yourself an edge using this five-point program:

1. Set a direction by identifying your missions and goals.

2. Develop plans to achieve those goals.

3. Find allies who are willing to help.

4. Go for healthy rewards.

5. Measure your progress and adjust your direction based on what you discover.

I'll explain each of these elements in the following sections. Then, in the next few chapters, we'll look at how you can apply the Five-Point Program to specific kinds of change.

Step 1: Set a Direction

Your first step is to decide what change you want to achieve; this is your direction. You can start by picking a personal challenge or an item from the genie's list. If necessary, start with a sketchy direction. You can flesh it out as you go along.

IDENTIFY YOUR MISSION

To give a deeper meaning to your direction, add a mission statement. This is your vision translated into words.

Your mission begins with a simple statement made of two aims: (1) to do something constructive and (2) to accomplish a specific result. These two elements apply to missions developed by corporations, religions, political parties, and people like you and me.

Let's look at a classic mission. The mission of India's famous religious leader, Mahatma Gandhi, was (1) to propel India toward independence from Great Britain and (2) to prepare the people of India for self-rule. Armed with this mission, Gandhi focused on getting the British out of India so the people could govern themselves. Of course, he had a basic plan to achieve the mission: passive noncooperation. He believed that when the Indian people refused to cooperate with the British, the British would not have enough resources to carry on the responsibilities of government.

Not all missions are constructive. Some are perverse, illegal, and destructive. For example, Chicago crime boss Al Capone's expressed mission was (1) to bootleg booze and (2) to bring pleasure to people's lives. Although he may have brought some pleasure to some people's lives, he also brought death and destruction. Capone's mission statement was a rationalization to justify criminal behavior.

Your healthy personal mission may be to (1) develop your perspective, confidence, and tolerance and (2) improve the quality of your choices. To achieve your mission, you resolve to make responsible efforts, then you act on that resolve.

SET GOALS

You define your mission based on the direction you intend to take. Your goals define the specific steps you'll take in pursuit of the mission. As you meet each goal, you go forward to the next goal in line. Like railroad stations, each goal is a temporary stopover point. For example, if your mission is to develop writing skills, your goals might be to (1) practice writing, (2) get feedback from an instructor or expert, (3) apply those suggestions to the next set of practice writings, (4) get more feedback, and so on. Like all achievable goals, these are specific and measurable.

Goals have boundaries, as the following examples show:

- As general of the Air Force, your wartime goal is to protect your country's civilian population and resources and to destroy your opponent's ability to wage war. To achieve your goal, you take action to disable the enemy's communications, destroy the enemy command, disable the opponent's military and air capabilities, and destroy industry vital to your enemy's war efforts. But your two-part goal has boundaries that limit what you can or will do. The boundary conditions include minimizing civilian casualties, maintaining political support, reducing the risk of casualties to your forces and losses of your equipment, securing the most able strategic performers in your high command, ensuring the highest quality of training for your pilots, maintaining contingency plans, and so forth. The decisions you make will reference these boundary conditions to your mission and goals.

- As an entrepreneur starting your own small business, your goals may be to ensure that you have the management skills to hire, market, maintain controls, secure adequate financing, and sell the services and products you supply. The boundary conditions may include ensuring that your family has adequate care, that you operate within regulation and law, that your products and services are safe, and that the changes you make support the viability and profitability of your enterprise.

- As a self-changer, your goals may include (1) identifying, developing, and using your strengths, and (2) recognizing and overcoming inner impediments (false beliefs, nonproductive uses of time, problem habits, and stressful emotions such as depression and anxiety). Your boundary conditions may include not needlessly harming others, reflecting before acting, supporting long-term growth over temporary inconvenience, ensuring good physical health, and avoiding risk that heightens your chances of injury.

Boundary conditions are important points to consider because they take both your values and your missions into consideration. When you know the boundaries and are clear on your goals, you will find it easier to make focused decisions.

You set goals as a prelude to advancing your interests. Sighting beyond your goals can add thrust to your ability to achieve them. Suppose you set a goal of completing a 26.5-mile marathon. You might train for the race by running two hours every other day to prepare yourself to finish that specific distance. But what if you had sights beyond that goal? You might then practice by training to run a 40-mile race. The extra training could instill a different mental attitude about the marathon: 26.5 miles may not feel so long. You might even finish the race with energy to spare! Now, I'm not recommending that you train to run 40 miles to compete effectively in a 26.5-mile marathon. Rather, consider this a concrete example of reaching beyond your goal.

When you look forward to what lies beyond the goal, you see

the goal as a station by the track to your next change. This is an important growth perspective.

Step 2: Make Plans

Your mission determines the direction of change. Your goals tell you what stations you will pass on the way. Your plans tell how to get to each station in ways that are consistent with your goals and boundaries.

A plan prescribes how you will organize your efforts. It outlines the tools, methods, and processes you will use to arrive at your destination. A well-conceived plan answers these questions:

- Where am I now?
- Where am I going?
- What do I need to do to get there?
- What other routes are available?

Plans that work have several common features: They are objective and future-focused; they are simple, yet complete; they are elastic in that you can change them as circumstances warrant.

How can you structure a detailed yet simple plan that leads directly toward your goal? Following are two techniques.

THE BRAINSTORMING TECHNIQUE

Brainstorm with yourself. In the initial planning phases, you can play "what if" games. Think about possible challenges, obstacles, and opportunities. Imagine dealing with each one. Play out the plan in your mind.

THE BACKWARD PLAN TECHNIQUE

Make a backward plan. We usually plan steps in sequence; we decide what will happen first, second, third, and so on. You also can plan the opposite way—working your plan backward from your desired result.

To make a backward plan, you picture a goal and then imagine you have already achieved it. Then pretend you are looking back at what you did. Ask yourself what step you took just before you met the goal. What was the step before that?

Working backward is a Zen concept. The Zen master tries to hit the bull's-eye with an arrow. So he draws his bow and points it toward the target. Before releasing the arrow, he imagines it centered in the bull's-eye. Next he pictures the arrow coming back in space to its seat on the drawn bowstring. He adjusts his aim based on the imagined trajectory. When everything feels in place, he releases the string and the arrow pierces the bull's-eye.

When you have clearly visualized the trajectory that leads back from your goal, you can make each backward step a part of your plan.

When it comes to planning, an axiom from famous basketball coach Bobby Knight applies: "It's not committing to win that's important. It's committing to prepare to win."

Step 3: Find Allies

Business research has shown that a group decision-making process can bring about positive change. The process works best when each group member feels a sense of ownership in the process. Psychotherapy research shows that people are more likely to make personal changes when they work with a knowledgeable, empathic, accepting person—or group—who gives constructive feedback.

Supportive people offer different perspectives. They may confirm some of your thinking, but they also may identify alternative routes you had not considered before. Where are you to find the most capable of these allies? It depends on the help you want. Your banker, for example, can help you judge if a business project would be profitable. A counselor or friend can help you judge your strengths and limitations. The local librarian can show you how to find information. A stranger can give directions to the street you seek in a new town. A collaborator can help on a shared project.

Here are some potential allies for your change program:

- Your mate, a lifelong friend, a close relative, members of your social circle, business partners, and colleagues.

- People you have met in industry organizations, civic groups, religious institutions—any gathering of people who have convened to pursue a common interest or goal.

- Authors and thinkers. The editors of *Consumer Reports*, for example, can provide you with information on which products represent the greatest total value.

You also can put together a support group of people who, like you, want to power their development and are willing to share their resources. Working with such a group makes it far more likely that you will follow through on your change program.

Step 4: Seek Rewards

Rewards are the logical outcome of your change programs—things you have a legitimate right to work toward and expect for your labors. Your rewards are more than getting M&Ms or dollar bills for performing effectively.

A meaningful reward can be a powerful but subtle incentive for action. One lasting reward is the growing ability to use the skills and understanding you gain from pursuing change.

Rewards are strong incentives, to be sure, but they can work against you in a subtle way. Suppose you never reach your goals because you repeatedly cause yourself to fail? Well, are you getting an unexpected reward? You may have to look hard to find it, but it is there somewhere. Perhaps your reward for causing yourself to fail is the attention or sympathy you get if you lament about your plight.

Psychological research has shown that a short-term reward will increase the frequency of a behavior it follows. That includes behavior that many of us view as self-defeating. For example, some people behave neurotically and defeat themselves by alienating others. After years of poor results you'd think they would stop, since they have won no visible benefits. Or have they? In reality, there are rewards at work driving the neurotic behavior. They are secondary gains. For instance, the self-defeating person may get attention or avoid painful imaginary foes. Thus, when attention—even angry attention—follows a neurotic response, the person is likely to repeat it. Although few of us engage in such extreme undertakings, there is a message: You are wise to look carefully at what rewards you receive and why you receive them.

Be sure that the rewards offered by the Five-Point Change Program are healthy. They can be internal: enjoying a feeling of self-efficacy. They can be external: receiving love, trophies, money— anything that reinforces your sense of accomplishment. They can be abstract: gaining justice, freedom, or loyalty.

Self-change can involve long periods marked by frustration and discouragement. Yet, when we set our sights on specific rewards, we can ignore moment-to-moment discomforts as we strive to fulfill our higher visions and missions. Thus, when we work toward obtaining desired and attainable goals, we often override temporary disadvantages and build a strong will to go on.

Step 5: Measure Your Progress

How do you know how well you are doing with your change program? What are your criteria for success? How do the results of your plan measure against the objectives you have set?

You judge the quality of your results by the standards you set to measure the effect of your actions. When you meet a standard, you are successful. The standard can be subjective, such as achieving peace of mind or a sense of well-being.

Suppose your mission was to improve your ability to tolerate frustration. One measurement standard might then be your ability to remain clearheaded in frustrating situations. Thus, you are using "clearheaded" as an emotional barometer to measure your progress.

You can also use objective standards to rate your progress, adopting familiar measures such as a score of 93 percent or better, or receiving an "A" on an examination. You can then keep a box score on the results of your insights, predictions, and judgments, and thereby build a factual basis for assessing your judgments and actions. Are they "right" most of the time? Are you making progress on your change program?

As you formulate your set of standards, remember that the same ones don't apply to all of us. Olympic-class athletes, for example, practice six or more hours a day to develop and refine their skills to near-perfection. At world-level competition, the standards for success are unique. Does that mean that if you enjoy athletic competition you must meet world-class standards? Hardly! You can set your standard for the skill level you want to enjoy. Figure out what goal is reasonable for you, then get to it!

Are standards carved in stone? If the measurement of your progress shows that you are falling short of your goals, perhaps it's time to take stock and make some changes in the plans you are using to achieve your goals. If this happens, you have three basic choices:

1. Develop a "new" strategy. One young entrepreneur wanted to start a business and went in search of a retired person to show her the ropes. Within a matter of weeks she recognized that such generosity was hard to find, and she formed a new plan for learning about starting a business.

2. Change your standards. You may have set unrealistic criteria. You may have over- or underrated your strengths. If so, you will need to adjust your standards or reassess your strengths.

3. Quit. Some people believe that quitting means failure, but quitting makes sense if the cost of continuing is too high. Consider quitting if your plan is doing more harm than good or if you've selected a goal that is beyond your reach—such as trying to shoot an arrow two miles when your range is a few hundred yards! Also, circumstances can change. In such an instance, quitting your present plan is a legitimate choice, provided that you base your decision on a careful assessment of present and future conditions.

Your measures also help you remember where you are going, learn how far you can stretch, and find your breakpoint for different challenges. What could be more important than to know when to continue, change direction, or stop?

POSTSCRIPT

The world is a chaotic place, but it is the only place in which we live. You can try to avoid this chaos, but your efforts will avail you nothing. Better to take advantage of chaos and change; they are natural teachers. Learning to respond effectively to these changes enables you to flourish.

Your best chance in a chaotic world lies in shaping your resources for change. You can boost your self-development chances when you direct your efforts toward an important and achievable end, when you create and control opportunities, and when you take advantage of unexpected events. You may not change the world, but you can make your life better using the Five-Point Change Program.

In the following chapters I will discuss how to apply the Five-Point Program to psychological problems and how to use psychological principles to boost the effectiveness of this self-management system. Test it. Perhaps you will find ways to refine and use the program and go beyond what I have written in this book.

8

Changing Problem Habits

Problem habits rank high on the list of items that most people want to change about themselves. Do you feel frustrated because you have a problem habit you want to stop? Do you want to quit worrying, smoking, eating too much, daydreaming, complaining, withdrawing, or avoiding? If you are like practically every other human on this planet, you habitually do something you'd be better off skipping. In this chapter you'll learn how the Five-Point Program applies to changing problem habits.

WHAT MAKES A HABIT A PROBLEM?

The ways we eat, brush our teeth, and tie our shoes are habit patterns. You develop these habits when you repeat a sequence until it occurs without much forethought. These habits are not problems. They perform the positive function of freeing your mind from tedious detail. They promote efficiency. If people couldn't develop habits and follow predictable routines, you would not be reading this book and I could not have written it.

Problem habits have nothing to do with efficiency. They are rooted in your mind, chemistry, and muscles. They are the result of complex processes that can vary from person to person and with age, stage of development, and gender. They vary in strength from inconvenient and readily changeable to serious, stubborn, and entrenched. They are part of an interconnected labyrinth of well-practiced subhabits and, in some cases, neural and hormonal inter-actions that cause a physical urge. They frequently provide quick (but temporary) relief from tension. Some, like compulsive nail bit-ing, might grow out of tension but can continue after tense times pass. They evolve into highly practiced patterns of behavior that come to exist on their own.

WHY ARE PROBLEM HABITS SO HARD TO CHANGE?

When temporarily deprived of an addictive substance, the affected person goes into a state of withdrawal (shakes, irritability, preoccu-pation with the substance) and often feels desperate to consume the substance and quell the withdrawal sensations.

When your appetite for the substance starts to swell like an electrical surge, you may experience a strong, sometimes sudden, pressure. This attention-grabbing inner emotional or physical force prompts you to satisfy your habit urges. The surge stops temporar-ily when you satisfy the hunger.

It is tough to resist the inner call of problem habit urges, par-ticularly for addictive substances once you have developed a dependency for their chemical effects. The compelling urge comes from a very primitive part of our human brain where we have a sort of reptile mentality that seeks immediate satisfaction of its appetites. These strong inner presses and drives follow a rudimen-tary route that largely bypasses our logical circuits. For example, instead of the nutritional food we know we need, we guzzle booze, chain-smoke, or chomp down on one potato chip after another as if we were driven to store fat for winter hibernation. Now, our intel-lectual circuits serve the function of satisfying the primitive urge to consume by finding ways to obtain the substance of choice.

Our primitive drives have been around longer than our logic.

They are very powerful. That's why we can't snap our fingers and change. Indeed, the purpose of our intellect is to secure advantage in economically obtaining goods for our survival. That is why our *educated reason* is often an afterthought or serves to support and justify the habit. Yet educated reason is our best hope for change. Through the process of educated reasoning we can piece together the consequences of indulging in our problem habits and take the necessary steps to change. Millions have succeeded in kicking their unwanted habits; some with the help and support of others, some on their own.

The founders of Rational Recovery, Jack and Lois Trimpey, contend that people with addictive behaviors have an addictive voice that wheedles, cons, or compels them to act to satisfy their addictive urge. People who train themselves to recognize this addictive voice give themselves the choice to confront this inner con and overcome their addictive behavior. Like cockroaches exposed to the light, these change-resistant addictive cons can vanish under the illuminating power of reason. Unfortunately, they will lurk in the background in readiness to reappear when reason dims or neglects its duty; eternal vigilance is the price of freedom.

BREAKING PROBLEM HABITS

Most people try to use restraint to stop problem habits because it seems like the intuitively correct thing to do. Yet, restraint involves control, suppression, and strain—the very things that cause double troubles and snafu our best change intentions.

Except in few cases, this straightjacketing technique doesn't work. For example, the majority of people who want to lose weight use restraint when they diet. Most of them eventually gain back more than they lost. Also, restraint doesn't work for the smokers who say they want to quit but keep relapsing.

Why is restraint so inefficient? Chances are that you will feel uptight because you are straining to restrain yourself. The extra stress fuels thoughts of habit relief. You engage the habit when you believe you must have that relief now!

An alternate habit change strategy involves developing an "easy" attitude toward the problem habit. With this easy attitude,

you allow yourself to experience the habit discomfort without gri-
macing and tensing to avoid the urge. When you allow yourself to
experience the habit pressures, study them, and follow what happens to them, you are better able to live past them. That is because:
(1) They cease to be a mystery as you better understand their
undulating quality; (2) you learn that by accepting the urge, that
act transforms the urge into feelings you can tolerate; (3) you have
more space to exercise your will to change.

A will to change is different than restraint. Restraint is a
"white knuckle" effort at control. A will to change is a commanding
effort that often starts to grow from a flickering desire. This desire
prompts experimenting with the change. These experiments can
cause an ever-increasing involvement with and commitment to the
change. And although such a change in process can include *some*
white knuckling, a will to change more importantly involves direction, intention, and measured action.

In this Five-Point Change Program, let's look at alternative
ways to build a will to change in order to break problem habits.

Step 1: Set a Direction

Let's assume that your mission is to break a problem habit. Part of
breaking problem habits involves learning to accept temporary discomfort in the service of getting bigger, long-term gains. If you
have high frustration tolerance you will be at a lower risk for
indulging problem habits, because you will be able to accept
unpleasant experiences and feelings, delay gratification, and maintain self-control in trying circumstances. Therefore, your goal is to
build high frustration tolerance.

Step 2: Make Plans

Frustration tolerance development partially involves shifting your
perspective from believing that you *must* satisfy your urges to feeling confident that you can master the techniques that allow you to
delay gratification. Consider that when you have poison ivy,

scratching where it itches spreads the itch. Although scratching may be immediately satisfying, you don't have to scratch every time you feel an itch. You can use calamine lotion, mow the lawn, read a book, or absorb yourself in other activities. You develop frustration tolerance. Eventually the itch goes away.

You can break problem habits in the same way by deflecting your attention from the habit onto something more productive. This technique is part of your plan. For example, you might keep a pitcher of ice water in the refrigerator. When you have a habit urge, slowly sip two eight-ounce glasses of the water. Wait five minutes. If you still have the urge, have another glass of water. For problem habits you may need to try several plans. Often the habit runs so deep that replacement alone is not enough, and getting to the root of the habit is the best plan. Following are some techniques to help you advance your plan.

THE STOP-REFLECT-ACT TECHNIQUE

Although the motives behind habits and their degree of severity vary, certain factors contribute to the stimulation or the continuation of all problem habits. They are:

- Associating particular cues with the habit

- Allowing yourself to slide into a trance state where you "mindlessly" follow your habit urges

- Sensing pleasure or satisfaction in acting out the habit

- Making excuses, rationalizations, and paper-thin explanations to justify continuing the habit

- Feeling ambivalent over the change—that is, of breaking the habit

- Feeling stressed

- Letting a feeling of helplessness grow out of your sense that your change efforts are futile

- Engaging in negative self-talk over disappointing progress in changing the habit

- Blaming others or circumstances for your problem habit

- Copying someone else's problem habit patterns

When you change one or more of these conditions, you weaken your problem habit. To change any one of these, follow the stop-reflect-act technique. Start with recognizing the cues that connect with your habit urge so you are prepared to (1) *Stop* and listen to your inner voice that stirs the habit (i.e., "Come on, let's do it. What's the harm?"), (2) *Reflect* by reminding yourself to slow down and think of alternative actions, and (3) *Act* to execute alternative actions. With continuous practice, you make this stop-reflect-act technique into a habit.

THE INNER DIALOGUE TECHNIQUE

Knowing what to do and doing it are not the same thing. Don Meichenbaum, a cognitive-behavioral psychologist at the University of Waterloo in Canada, and his colleagues have looked at the reasons people give themselves for continuing problem habits and for not following through with what are generally thought of as healthy habits. These psychologists observed that many don't make the effort to change because they question whether such behaviors are worthwhile for them, because they focus too much on the barriers to change, or because they have other, more deep-seated personal reasons (e.g., a lack of will, a fatalistic outlook, etc.).

Meichenbaum stresses that if you are going to change self-defeating parts of your behavior, then you had better listen to your inner dialogue—that is, pay attention to what you tell yourself. What you tell yourself can influence how you feel and what you do, and what you do also can influence what you tell yourself. Meichenbaum has outlined a problem-solving self-instructional approach that you can employ after you first have the impulse to indulge your problem habit and before you would normally consummate the habit.

Because we don't always think before we act, it is wise to prepare deflecting behaviors in advance. Think about what you want to accomplish, then verbally guide yourself through the process.

For example, instead of promising yourself that you are simply going to stop indulging a problem habit, give yourself specific instructions to do something different when the urge arises. Then follow these instructions.

Suppose you want to stop your habit of eating foods that are fattening. When faced with a strong desire for a bowl of ice cream, you normally might indulge yourself. To defeat the habit, you prepare a set of instructions to follow when the urge strikes. You start by defining what you want to accomplish: In this case, you want to eat more healthfully. Tell yourself to go to the refrigerator, then make and eat a salad following precise, prescribed steps: "I am going to go to the refrigerator and take out lettuce, tomatoes, carrots, and celery. I am going to prepare a salad by mixing these ingredients in a bowl. I will use my favorite low-fat creamy garlic dressing for flavoring." When the ice cream pressure swells, carry out the instructions. The salad may not taste as delicious as a bowl of ice cream, but the process of carrying out your own instructions can buy time until the habit urge passes.

Meichenbaum suggests that you first say these instructions out loud, next whisper them to yourself, and then repeat them silently. That procedure helps reinforce the message and defuses the immediacy of satisfying your problem habit urges.

When you follow this coping method, you show yourself that you can change a problem habit because you can exercise control over the outcome. You now have another choice besides giving in to the habit. You have demonstrated that you can change your thoughts and activities to effectively override problem habit urges by adapting and using functional new ways of thinking and acting.

Meichenbaum's approach allows you to become your own change coach. You identify short-term behavior goals, articulate a game plan, anticipate barriers, make public commitment statements to others, reinforce yourself for trying, anticipate possible lapses, and prepare a back-up plan in case you backslide.

Applying his technique is not as simple as it may sound. It requires making a plan and pursuing thoughtful follow-up action. This takes time. Still, Meichenbaum's change strategy provides a solid guideline for anyone who is serious about changing unwanted habits or developing functional new ones.

PLANS FOR SPECIFIC HABITS

Along with the general habit-breaking techniques, your plans may be specific to the habit you are trying to break. Two habits that top the list of harmful habits are smoking and overeating. Here are some tips that you can try working into your plan to break either of these harmful habits.

For Smoking:

- If you want to quit smoking "cold turkey," then stop smoking and plan on staying off cigarettes forever.

- If cold turkey doesn't work for you, change your habit patterns as a prelude to quitting: Replace your brand of cigarettes with a brand lower in tar and nicotine; gradually decrease to zero the percentage of the time you inhale; use food coloring to put a circle on your cigarettes, and smoke only to that circle. Each day, ratchet the circle closer to the top.

- Join a smoke stoppers' support group.

- Graph the cost of smoking on a chart by making daily entries of the amount of money you spend on cigarettes.

- Wrap your cigarettes in a package and put them in your freezer. Whenever you believe you must smoke, unbundle the package and take out an individual cigarette. Then rewrap the remainder of the cigarettes and put them back into the freezer.

- Make a question card and keep it in your wallet. Include such questions as: (1) Do I want to get cancer from smoking? (2) Why can't I stand the discomfort of quitting? (3) If I don't smoke this cigarette right now, what is the worst thing that can happen? (4) Is it possible for me to hold off lighting up for five minutes? Ask and answer each question whenever you have an urge to smoke.

- When you feel an urge to light a cigarette, divert yourself into another activity, such as washing your hands, filing materials, or doing your exercises.

- Once you have stopped, avoid lulling yourself into restarting by assuming you can smoke a pipe or cigar once in a while. Such actions will cause the nicotine habit to kick in again at full strength.

For Overeating:

If you want to maintain your weight at a desired level, use what I call a lifetime "no-diet" diet plan for weight control. On this lifetime plan, you follow a nutritionally wise eating pattern, enabling you to slowly lose weight until you level off at your ideal weight. (Discuss the nutrition and ideal weight with your doctor.) You won't have to change your diet at that point because you have already changed it. The following can be worked into your plan to help support the change in your eating:

- Don't stock fattening foods such as cakes, cookies, potato chips, and other non-essential snack or dessert items.

- Drop one fattening component from your diet each month. Pick the most fattening first (ice cream or cake, for example).

- Try a moderate- to low-fat eating routine that provides all the essential nutrients. Discuss with your doctor how much fat you should consume.

- With a low-fat eating plan, you will be able to develop a large variety of tasty alternate foods: Choose London broil or chicken sautéed with "no-fat" salad dressing, or your favorite fish instead of marbled beef; substitute no-fat sherbet for ice cream; try fruit bars instead of chocolate chip cookies.

- Make a written contract with a friend who wants to both lose weight and keep it off. Have the contract specify how you will lose the weight as well as your desired outcome.

- Chew slowly. Savor your food in small bites. Slow down the tempo of eating and enjoy your food more. This pacing also tends to cut consumption.

Step 3: Find Allies

Support is very important in any change area, but it can be particularly helpful for defeating problem habits. Make sure that the allies you choose really want to help you effect the change and do not sabotage your efforts. Try to find someone with a similar habit who is also committed to changing it.

Step 4: Seek Rewards

You can reward yourself in any way that works for you, *except indulging the habit as your reward*. If you reward yourself for eating healthfully by having a hot fudge sundae, you are sabotaging your efforts. Your reward for eating healthfully would be that you feel fit and have more energy, and may have lost weight. Your reward for not biting your nails could be seeing your nails look neat and trim. Look for the positive results of your action—and enjoy them.

Step 5: Measure Your Progress

Problem habits are usually the easiest to measure because they are quantifiable. If you have stopped or cut back on smoking, you can count fewer cigarettes smoked. You can see this result. If you have stopped saying "Uh" between every few words, perhaps people have begun to respond more favorably to your presentations or conversations.

Now try tailoring your own Five-Point Change Program to help get rid of your problem habit.

1. What is your direction?

2. What are your plans?

3. Who are your allies?

4. What are your rewards?

5. How is your progress measured?

POSTSCRIPT

We are genetically programmed to eat, reproduce, protect ourselves, and survive. We are like all lower forms of animals in this respect. But we stand apart in that we can predict the consequences of our actions. We can also, therefore, intentionally take steps to avoid unpleasant results. That mental power gives us all hope for change! But exercising these options is far more easily said than done.

Consider this: Self-initiated change normally results from a deliberate and sustained effort where you make a commitment to change your habit behavior, not your habit urges.

9

Making Emotional Changes

E motions flow like birds in flight, which go to different lows and different heights. They trigger and inhibit change. Some provoke activity. Others drag like lead balls. Once you know the different causes and sources of emotions, you can enhance your ability to manage the most arduous of transformations with increased confidence.

The more you understand your emotions, the better you can appreciate the ways and whys of what you and others do. In this chapter we'll look at emotions: what they are and what they have to do with change.

EMOTIONAL CATALYSTS

If you didn't have emotions, your existence would lose all meaning and you would live a dry, passionless, robot life. Without your emotions, you might not thrive or survive because you'd have no sense of love or fear. Still, explaining these mercurial spirits is like describing what music sounds like and how each member of an orchestra plays a part in the performance of a symphony.

Emotions are not mysterious. We know they come from these main sources:

- Archetypal images imprinted on our brains, which respond to sensory information and primitive perceptions. Without this preprogramming, would we know to flee or fight? These imprints also influence who attracts and repels us. They are our primary emotions.

- Our biochemistry, which stimulates the brain. Hormones and neurochemicals activate many physical responses, such as a quickened heartbeat and sweaty palms.

- Our affective beliefs, images, and thinking. These cognitive processes are secondary signaling systems that trigger emotions. Our emotions also evoke thoughts associated with those emotions.

Our emotions mostly rise from perceptions and thought. If you feel emotionally attracted toward a work of art, the work has the evocative power to stir your emotions.

Emotions can signal crooked thinking and mislead the individual who experiences them. The irrationally jealous husband who assumes that all men are actively trying to take his wife from him probably has his faulty beliefs in control of his emotional facilities. The emotions are real enough, but he supports his case with incorrect assumptions and misinterpretations of reality. If we are to change our emotions, we have to understand the two types: primary and secondary.

Primary Emotions

Primary emotions, such as fear, abandonment, and love, have archetypal roots. They erupt when evoked by thoughts or events powerful enough to trigger them. Here are some examples:

- If you saw Freddy Kruger charging you, you'd feel fear and flee, or feel anger and fight. You'd feel a rush as adrenaline rams through your body and your pulse quickens, muscles contract, and breathing accelerates.

- Suppose you grew up in a primitive tribe whose members could only communicate through grunts and signs, and one day you woke up to find that the tribe had packed their tents and left you behind. You would no doubt feel abandoned.

- If you see an attractive person you may feel moonstruck, faint of heart, on top of the world, nervous, obsessed, and possessed. Would you say you felt "in love" or that your "brain was saturated with the love chemicals phenyleth-ylamine (PEA) and oxytocin"? These and other brain opiates, such as endorphins, influence a wide range of interpersonal emotions, including attachment.

Primary emotions transmit from your perceptions, through the emotional centers in your brain, down to your body, and then return full cycle to color your perceptions.

Secondary Emotions

Your emotional pool starts to get muddy as soon as you develop thought and language and misconceptions. These factors, perhaps, are what make some emotional conditions complex and tough to understand.

As our thoughts evolve, the tones of our emotions commingle with our inborn feelings and generate over 500 hybrid emotions. Although we don't need language to emote, our language gives special content and coloring to our emotions. These verbal hybrids include feelings of concern, joviality, desperation, cheer, urgency, merriment, embarrassment, joy, loneliness, gaiety, anxiety, happiness, guilt, contentment, regret, serenity, disappointment, trust, and hope. All of these are secondary emotions.

Our beliefs play a powerful role in those verbal sensations we call emotions. When a negative thought ("I am a worthless failure") follows an undesired performance, this belief generates inferiority feelings. You might even cower in submission before this idea, as an ancient relative might have done in the presence of a pack leader.

Verbal and visual images evoke primary emotions such as fear. If your friends are overdue, you may feel afraid because you can imagine them in an accident. We also generate emotions through the sensory imagery of music, poetry, drama, and art.

We create emotions through the images we conjure up in our minds. Method actors have known this for centuries: If you want to feel angry, reconstruct an angry event in your mind. You can also act out pleasant emotions and constructive habits and use these experiments to build confidence in yourself as a changemaker.

BUILDING EMOTIONAL MIGHT

Like mixing cream and sugar into a cup of tea, primary emotions blend with secondary emotions and drives. When you separate the mix, you can get a better handle on what is happening within you. Let's apply the Five-Point Change Program to the task of building emotional strength.

Step 1: Set a Direction

Your emotions are part of your make-up. You can't choose to eliminate them, but you can choose to develop your inner emotional resources. Let's see how.

Let's assume that you want to experience certain emotions— for example, joy—more often. Start with your mission. To decide how to evoke the emotions you wish to experience, ask yourself these questions:

- What thoughts—ideas or images—fit with the emotions I want to experience?

- What conditions are conducive to these emotions?

These questions suggest that you can, within your abilities and resources, create conditions and generate the psychological environment to fit with the types of emotions you want to experience.

Once you have found your mission, we next turn to the goals—the *hows* and *whats*—of experiencing.

Our first goal is to accept our emotions for what they are. You may think that acceptance means feeling neutral about frustrating or unpleasant events. However, acceptance means recognizing reality for what it is. With acceptance you feel what is there to feel. This act alone helps you tolerate or change conditions you don't like. It enables you to know when the best form of change is to learn to act differently or to grimly acknowledge that there are certain conditions that can't be changed, such as growing older.

As much as you might want to, you cannot avoid natural emotions such as sadness and frustration. When you accept these emotions for what they are, you simultaneously accept yourself for who you are. Here acceptance means experiencing your emotions without judging them.

The second goal is allowance. This means you permit you to be you. Allow yourself to have strengths as well as frailties and accept your experiences for what they are.

Step 2: Make Plans

Does reading ten books on how to drive an automobile make you an expert driver? Definitely not! You can learn from a book where to put the key, how to steer your car, how to make a right turn, and other aspects of the mechanics of driving. You can, in other words, plan or prepare to drive successfully, but you can develop driving skill only by driving.

Similarly, you can't completely plan your emotions, but you can plan to create conditions that generate what you'd like to experience. You can, for example, plan to meet people who are most gratifying to know. You can plan to broaden and deepen your emotional knowledge. Following are several emotional concepts and exercises you can use to help develop your emotional strength.

THE EMOTIVE VOCABULARY TECHNIQUE

A well-developed emotive vocabulary is an important tool for identifying and understanding the thoughts behind your feelings.

An emotive vocabulary is a word pool for labeling how you feel. For instance, if you are able to recognize and describe your feeling as "frustration" rather than "annoyance," you will think and act differently. In one case, you feel "thwarted"; in the other, "harassed." When you make this distinction, you are less likely to misunderstand yourself or your situation, and you will be able to act more effectively.

To build your emotive vocabulary, start a feelings log. The feelings log is a device you use to catalogue your feelings. In this log, describe your noteworthy experiences and the feelings and thoughts that accompany these events. Record your emotions, but don't judge them! Your perceptions may be true or false, but your feelings are true to your perceptions. They appropriately signal what you are perceiving or thinking. If anything, your thinking— or something else—may be off.

True, keeping a log can be a chore and a bore, but it is a surprisingly effective way to add to your emotional awareness. It will help you see value in accepting primary emotions such as sadness and in unraveling complex emotions such as jealousy. Understanding your emotions and perceptions is a worthy goal because as you increase your knowledge, you increase your awareness of what is important to you.

THE NAME-THAT-FEELING STRATEGY

This strategy will help you identify your emotions and how to express them. Emotions radiate changes to your exterior:

1. Expressions—laughing, frowning, blushing, "glowing"

2. Voice changes—smooth, shaky, extra loud, barely audible

3. Involuntary responses—sweating, muscles tense or relaxed, rapid or shallow breathing

4. Mannerisms—clenched fists, dropped jaws, clasped hands, open eyes

Our body speaks an emotional language. In a Walt Disney cartoon movie called *Johnny Fedora and Betty Blue Bonnet,* animated hats displayed emotional expression. For the hats, down-slanted eyes and down-turned brims indicated anger. Upturned eyes and turned-up brims showed pleasure. Cartoonist Walt Disney understood the universal signs of human emotions and used them with his animated characters.

Psychologist Paul Ekman (1985) says that your face can be a useful source of emotional information. In particular, your smile is a doorway to your emotions. The "felt" smile conveys pleasure. We see the "contempt" smile in disdainful tightening of the corners of the lips. In the "fear" smile the lip muscles pull horizontally toward the ears, conveying the person's sense of helplessness. We can add more smiles to the list. How about a plastic smile with mockery behind the mask? Are you showing your true emotions when you smile?

In this variation of the name-that-feeling strategy you'll need a partner.

- You and your partner take turns asking each other to name your real feelings about specific events, people, situations, or objects. The subjects of your questions can range from aardvark to zymurgy and can include love, war, heroes, green grass, trash, diaper rash, football, and homeless people. You can even say how you feel about your pet rock.

- Each person gets to ask the other 20 feeling questions, one question at a time. The respondent expresses a feeling within three seconds after each question. Then you reverse roles.

- Each person states real feelings: excited, warm, frustrated, disgusted, jealous, angry, joyful, anxious. Answers such as "I felt sarcastic" don't count. Sarcasm is a response to emotions such as anger or insecurity. Instead, use the feeling words *anger* or *insecure.*

- Exclude general emotional words such as *dislike, bad, good, pleasant,* and *unpleasant.* These terms artificially restrict your range of emotional expression.

- Exclude questions that ask for information: "How old are you?" "What kinds of automobiles do you prefer to drive?" Instead, ask, "What feeling comes to mind when you think about a new Cadillac?"

- Make no comment about the expressed feeling. Accept what you hear without expressing a judgment. The idea is to make this a positive experience, not an inquisition.

You may find this exercise more challenging than it first appears, especially when you have no strong emotional reaction to some conditions. You also may feel awkward and clumsy identifying and expressing your emotions. If so, practice; practice until expressing your emotions feels natural.

THE DISCRETIONARY MEANING TECHNIQUE

Irrational ideas are the source of many painful emotional states, such as depression. The ideas are discretionary when you can choose to think differently.

Some irrational ideas can pile misery upon misery. In that respect, people are worse off than cats. For example, a depressed cat probably would not care if it felt depressed for a day, a week, or a year. The cat lives from moment to moment and doesn't ponder how long any particular sensation will last. Unlike the cat, depressed people add to their miseries by appending evaluations, judgments, and unpleasant memories to their already sad plight. They focus on their sense of helplessness and hopelessness as they painfully experience the slow tick of time. In short, they add discretionary meaning to their physically stressed condition by talking to themselves about how badly they feel.

Discretionary meanings hurt in other ways. A person who has made a mistake is justified in regretfully saying, "I wish I had not done that." Others can give themselves a dose of inferiority feelings by adding, "I should have known better. I'm stupid, I can't do anything right." These descriptions are discretionary because blaming yourself will not alter the mistake or stop you from making errors.

There are other discretionary ideas that you can throw into your emotional stew. These disturbing ideas cover many themes: "It's unfair. I can't stand it. I'm a lousy creep. I can't stand myself. Everything is awful. I am falling to pieces. I'll go on feeling miserable forever. I can't cope." Self-deprecatory inner raps, like this one, also layer misery onto misery.

You can, however, reduce your emotional turbulence by applying the discretionary meaning technique. Start by identifying your discretionary ideas. List them. Then try to support them with facts.

The plan to find factual support for an idea that promotes harm may, at first, sound self-defeating. Why seek support for beliefs that promote harm? Simple. In science, you falsify a hypothesis when you show it is not true.

THE MOOD PERSPECTIVE TECHNIQUE

One way to control some emotions is to put our moods into perspective. Moods—a form of brain state—are a "gray" area of consciousness. Our lingering moods range from pleasure to melancholia, from detachment to engagement, from affability to belligerence. Sometimes events and thinking evoke the mood. Sometimes our biology evokes the mood. Some moods we happily receive, others we don't.

Your mood might come from what you ate, the phases of the moon, the barometric pressure, or your hormonal cycle. Your mood might reflect your temperament. Although you may not find the cause, you can accept the mood as a mood and thus avoid the type of emotional torrent that comes when you layer a problem onto a problem by blaming yourself or circumstances.

Psychologists Stanley Schachter and Jerome Singer (1962) demonstrated how people interpret neurochemical changes as emotional arousal. Schachter and Singer found that people injected with epinephrine (adrenaline) and forewarned of what to expect— pounding heart, facial flush—go about their business without distress because they recognize the symptoms as drug side-effects. Conversely, when the psychologists did not inform the injected subjects of the epinephrine symptoms, this group interpreted the physical sensations as an emotional arousal. When the uninformed subjects entered a room where paid actors acted angry, they mimicked the mood of the actors. On the other hand, when the informed group entered a room of "angry" actors, they were not influenced by the prevailing mood.

Suppose you wake up one morning feeling depressed. If there is no obvious reason to explain your mood, you might invent reasons. You may blame yourself ("I'm no good") or events ("I got kicked out of high school in 1976"). Your attempts at interpretation only add to your negative emotions.

You can use the mood perspective technique by acting like Schachter and Singer's informed subjects. You accept the sensations as side-effects of a temporary physical condition, and you go about your business. Fortunately, you also can reflect on the thoughts associated with your ambient moods and put these ambient thoughts into perspective by labeling them "ambient"—that is, related to your ambient mood. In this way you don't misinform yourself about your mood sensations.

Step 3: Find Allies

Where and how you get support is not as important as being able to distinguish between emotional support and dependency. Strong support that helps you develop your coping skills enhances self-sufficiency. With time, you can fend for yourself. You determine when that time has arrived. You control that choice. Conversely, the spirit of dependency is that you believe you can't do much of anything without help.

Potential allies are people you know who care for you and who are willing to listen. Sometimes they can help you clarify emotional reality just by hearing you out and reflecting your thoughts and your feelings.

Step 4: Seek Rewards

The rewards of emotional self-management are both obvious and elusive. Perhaps the richest reward is subtle. You will discover that emotional intensity does not have to have a balance.

By this, I mean that experiencing high levels of emotional involvement doesn't mean that we have to experience deep lows. For example, if you were to experience joy at a level of 10, you don't have to feel misery at minus 10 when challenged by unfortunate happenings.

In addition, you can experience pure sensations of sadness, regret, remorse, happiness, and joy. You need not mar your emotional make-up with anger, anxiety, and depression.

Step 5: Measure Your Progress

Suppose you've been a suppresser and have held back your feelings. When you develop your emotional resources, you may feel the emotional freedom to express your opinions and ideas in a way that feels right. The feedback you would receive from others may include "I never knew you felt that way" or "You somehow seem different."

If you've previously defended yourself with emotional outbursts or hysteria, then your new feedback may include "You seem more tolerant." Under these conditions, you may find people more willing to approach you.

You are likely to find that the quality of your experiences will be your most important feedback. If you accept your emotions, you'll feel better about what you do and better about yourself. You'll act more in congruence with reality. You can use an "emotional thermometer" to measure change, but I think you'll know where you stand without it.

Now it's your turn to tailor your Five-Point Program to develop the types of experiences you want to have.

1. What is your direction?

2. What are your plans?

3. Who are your allies?

4. What are your rewards?

5. How do you measure your progress?

POSTSCRIPT

We long for mates we can love. We roll down the water slide at the amusement park for an emotional thrill. We play golf, tennis, football, baseball, and soccer for the fun of it. We go to sad movies so we can cry. We listen to our favorite musical artist to get absorbed in the sound. We visit the museum to ponder the beautiful mysteries of art. We do it for the feeling.

We enjoy many of our feelings. Our emotions flow from our

perception of events, our ideas, and even our senses. Some emotions, such as sadness and grief, linger and play out in their own way and own time until they are but whispering memories. All these emotions are signs of change.

Emotions are understandable. You can't change natural emotions. But when you accept them as they are—without judgment—then you are not going to be afraid of your feelings, and are more likely to feel more emotional highs and fewer emotional lows. You can direct—even control—your secondary verbal emotions by shaping your thinking to fit that ever changing process we call reality. When you accept that you have power over discretionary feelings and drives, you can responsibly reduce their frequency and impact.

10

Changing Your Level of Stress

Stress is a matter of situation and of *perspective*. Whether you feel stressed or not depends on whether you see yourself in control or as defenseless and overwhelmed. For example, would you feel stressed at the sight of a 25-foot-long great white shark moving toward you in the water? What if you were a trained marine biologist watching the shark from a protective metal cage? Would you feel differently?

We cannot avoid stress. However, we can make it into either a positive, propellant force or a negative, destructive one.

P-STRESS AND D-STRESS

Stress invariably accompanies change. It becomes a propellant for positive action if you respond by pushing yourself to learn, adapt, and develop. This propellant stress (p-stress) stimulates culture, creativity, and accomplishment.

But some stresses are destructive (d-stress), and these can have deadly consequences. D-stresses such as lingering depression, resentment, anxiety, pressure, and raw-nerve tension can cause serious problems in health, loving, and living. They severely restrict the types and methods of changes you will be able to make. High levels of tension command attention and distract from self-development and discovery.

Sometimes the hand of change casts you as a reluctant actor on the stage of stress. However, some stresses are a normal part of your daily life. Your boss criticizes you after you've made your best effort. Your colleague interrupts you when you want to concentrate on your project. You get caught in traffic and miss the last jet to your favorite vacation spot. Still, if you have a way to cope—or think you will find a way even if no answer immediately pops into your mind—then you are more likely to perceive yourself as being in control, and you will feel less d-stress.

CONSEQUENCES OF D-STRESS

Stress can be uncomfortable when you feel tied up in knots. It becomes destructive when that feeling lingers and you experience a stress overload. Depending on your make-up, this destructive stress can cause high cholesterol, heart disease, depression, ulcers, attention and concentration deficiencies, memory loss, neurogenia (chronic fatigue), and other unpleasant symptoms. Some scientists think signs of aging may be a product of the cumulative effects of d-stress (but this is a controversial theory).

D-stress tops the list of serious health problems of our times. Ongoing d-stress keeps us in a continuous overdrive. Our bodies have evolved to expect and withstand occasional crisis, but not to be continually churned up. There is a price to pay for continuing emotional churning.

Stress costs. The American Psychological Association reports that between 50 and 70 percent of usual visits to primary care physicians are for medical complaints that relate to psychological problems. Still, the physician needs to rule out a physical basis for common stress conditions that include chronic fatigue, recurrent headaches, and gastrointestinal distress.

The costs of using general medicine facilities to treat psychological disorders are astronomical, amounting to billions of dollars each year. But dollar costs are minor compared to the failing health, strained lives, relationship problems, and loss of a feeling of well-being that these continually stressed people experience.

Tranquilizers, amphetamines, and antidepressants prescribed for psychological stress may temporarily cloak stress symptoms. But they do not eliminate stress. Instead, they evoke misconceptions, faulty beliefs, poor self-concepts, learned helplessness, unrealistic expectations, and irrational claims.

D-stress can affect our bodies in many ways, from gastrointestinal distress to cardiovascular dysfunction. Managing stress effectively, however, involves the perception of ourselves as being able to cope with the situations we are in. James Blascovich, a psychologist at New York State University at Buffalo, has presented important new research findings demonstrating that people who believe they have insufficient resources to cope in a problem-solving situation make a cognitive appraisal that can affect their cardiovascular functioning. Their peripheral vascular system constricts and the heart must work harder to get blood through the system. This is a medically unhealthy situation because, over a period of years of experiencing threat and stress, such tightening can lead to heart disease in people vulnerable to this dysfunction. Now, here is the positive side of this picture. Blascovich's research also shows that when you view a problem situation as a challenge (you believe you can actively cope with it), you are likely to experience increased myocardial efficiency and decreased vascular constriction. This means that your heart pumps more efficiently because blood goes through the system with less resistance.

Psychological change strategies and techniques can make a big difference in reducing the personal and physical costs of d-stress. Competent psychological counseling could significantly offset these "stress" costs and literally save billions of dollars in "stress visits" to primary care physicians. For example, a challenge perspective enables us to see most stressful situations as manageable, rather than threatening. Positive preventative mental health techniques and strategies (as found in this book) can shrink the risk of psychological and physical disorders caused by d-stress for those who learn to put these concepts to good use.

Psychological Symptoms of D-Stress

Some of us paste smiles on our faces to cover stress wrinkles. Others look critical or aloof to cover shyness and fears. Still others let the helplessness show through. What is the result of covering up or capitulating to d-stress? We change for the worse.

How do you know if you suffer from d-stress? You may do some of the following:

- Show signs of "learned helplessness" and avoid making decisions or solving problems

- Feel guilty or anxious and make mountains out of molehills

- Escape through drugs or alcohol

- Experience extreme emotional mood swings that lead to crying, angry outbursts, or withdrawal

- Feel blue and have trouble sleeping or sleep too much

- Have stomachaches and headaches, feel listless, and experience other unpleasant physical symptoms, such as dry mouth, that could have a psychological or physical cause

- Feel "burnt out," that is, have a persistent dread of your situation accompanied by fatigue and irritability

Your d-stress risk dramatically rises if you tend to brood, dwell on angry thoughts, or view yourself as impotent in dealing with many facets of life. Chronic d-stress symptoms come from such preoccupations. They are discretionary problems, because we choose to have them. We gain d-stress from a variety of causes, among them affluence (oddly enough), hostility and worry, and mental oppression.

Causes of D-Stress

Affluence. World conditions have never been so favorable. With fewer threats to worry about, what is the concern? Yet over the past 30 years we've heard claims from various influential people who say our electronic age is bristling with stress. Poet W. H. Auden called ours the "age of anxiety." Albert Camus said we lived in the "century of fear." Beyond that, we face fears of inadequacy, worries over our reputation, stressful thoughts, tedium, and apprehension about our health and images. These are afflictions of affluence, and we rarely suffer from them unless we have too much time on our hands.

Why are many of us plagued by tension and fear? Do we worry too much about our place in the universe? Do we become preoccupied with our frailties and frustrated aspirations and ignore our potential? Perhaps we have lost too many survival challenges and therefore lapse into lassitude or try to fill our existential voids with mindless activities.

People worry about an uncertain future, an endangered environment, nuclear attack, disease, accidents, and other tragedies. Some of these people might be projecting their exaggerated fears into the future. A preoccupation with an imagined bleak future may, however, indicate a present life devoid of meaningful constructive challenges. I call this form of d-stress *leisure stress* because you feel it when you lack challenge and your life seems like a long, dark journey beset with static and confusion or resentment and helplessness.

Hostility and Worry. Much d-stress comes from prolonged residence in negative emotional states, such as hostility and worry. For example, people with hostile Type A personalities are susceptible to coronary heart disease because of their resentful hard-driving lifestyles.

Unfortunately, chronic stress also results from worry patterns where we constantly fret and torment ourselves over possibilities. We create problems for ourselves when we lament over our safety, social status, emotional health, physical condition, love life, work, environment, and neighbors—when we decry the unfairness of life.

Are there other social causes for stress? Almost certainly. External threats such as political instability, social changes, AIDS, and economic chaos may elicit a well-placed apprehension, but they don't cause d-stress. Any deterioration of authority and a breakdown of trust will promote stress. An atmosphere characterized by administrative deceptions that foster distrust can seriously strain people who normally have the capacity to cope.

Oppression of the Mind. The most common form of d-stress occurs when certain psychological and mental conditions become acute. You see people who:

- Lack outlets for their strong emotions

- Fear intimacy and emotional closeness

- Have an insipid spiritual life

- Are preoccupied with appearances

- Are unable to accept—and let others see—their personal limitations

These conditions reflect inner conflicts. People are torn whether to express or hold back emotions, to play it safe or risk rejection, to feel free or maintain control, to express their real beliefs or mouth politically correct words, to avoid risks or experiment with change.

Behind d-stress we find many conflicts between imagination and reality that often involve one or more of several misconceptions: Life should be fair; you should have what you want; you should have complete control over who you want to be or what you want to do; what was shouldn't have been. To find the illusions behind your d-stress, look for some unreasonable expectations about life.

BUILDING P-STRESS SKILLS

When you see yourself as a person who can solve problems, you develop a sense of control and the confidence that you can handle stress. In this context, psychologist Richard Lazarus (1991) correctly points out that our appraisal of an emotionally stirring event will influence the quality of our emotions about that event as well as the actions we will take. Further, he declares that by making an accurate objective assessment of the emotional event, we position ourselves to anticipate, prepare for, and manage change. In so doing, we are better able to tolerate frustration and to define situations that appear overwhelming.

You can develop propellant p-stress skills in many other ways and add to your sense of control. One important way is through relaxation.

When you feel relaxed, your thinking is clear and fluid and you feel composed. You have trouble responding adaptively and flexibly when your mind gyrates with anxious thoughts and your body feels strained with tension. By applying the awareness and action methods from this book, you can do much to think with a relaxed mind. You can also learn to defuse stress by developing your relaxation response. Let's see how we would use the Five-Point Program to build p-stress resiliency through relaxation.

Step 1: Set a Direction

A sound anti-d-stress mission is to use relaxation to lessen the effects of stress so that you can concentrate your efforts on meeting challenges. Following are four methods that you can use to help you achieve the mission:

- Develop muscle-relaxation skills.

- Use a simple concentration method to put your mind at rest.

- Develop an alternative relaxation method to add variety to your program.

- Combine relaxation with action to meet challenges.

Step 2: Make Plans

A useful plan would be to use strategies and techniques that build relaxation into your program for change. I'll go through several, each with a different aim. The physical relaxation system is designed to develop muscle-relaxation skills. The meditation approach is intended to put your mind at rest. The mental relaxation system seeks to develop pleasant images to calm your body and alternative relaxation methods to add variety to your program. These methods provide platforms for relaxed action.

THE PHYSICAL RELAXATION STRATEGY

Joseph Wolpe (1969), who developed behavior therapy, uses a muscle-relaxation method as part of his program to help people overcome their fears and phobias. Wolpe's system is an outgrowth of Edmond Jacobson's (1934) work on relaxation.

The muscle-relaxation system is simple. First find a comfortable chair to sit in—or you can lie down. Next, squeeze a muscle and tense it for about five seconds. Then slowly release that tension over the next five seconds. The rhythmic squeezing and the releasing of tension in various muscle groups eventually lead to a progressive relaxation.

Here are the steps:

- Tighten and then relax your right hand by making a fist, holding the tension, then letting the muscles in your hand and fingers go limp. Do the same with your left hand.

- Close both sets of fingers into loose fists. Turn your wrists toward the floor until the muscles feel tense. Release the tension.

- Hold your hands out with your palms down. Stretch out your fingers and turn them upward to put tension on the muscles in your palms and wrists. Let the muscles go droopy and loose.

- Close both hands and make fists. Keep your forearms parallel with the floor, then bend your fists toward the floor and put tension on your forearms. Let go of the tension.

- Shake your wrists, letting your fingers flop to loosen them. Then rotate your wrists slowly while tensing them. Let your wrists go limp and loose.

- Straighten your arms and tense your triceps. Release the tension.

- Tighten your biceps by turning your elbows up as though you were pulling up a heavy weight to your chest. Let your arms return to your sides as you release the pressure.

- Put your arms in a comfortable position and allow them to feel droopy and heavy. Imagine the strain in your arms melting like butter on a warm day.

- Tilt your head back and put gentle pressure on the muscles at the back of your neck. Straighten your head and relax the muscles.

- Bend your head forward until your chin touches your chest. This will put gentle pressure on the muscles at the back and front of your neck. Let your head return to a comfortable position.

- Gently rotate your head in a circular motion and slowly bring the movement to a stop.

- Wrinkle your forehead. Let the muscles slowly go limp and loose like a sack of flour. You may feel your eyebrows drooping down as you relax.

- Frown and feel your brow crease. Let the tension flow out as you let your brow return to normal.

- Close your eyes and tense your eyelids while keeping the rest of your face relaxed. Keep your eyelids closed and relax the tension.

- Clench your jaw. You may press your teeth together enough to create tension. Experience the tension. Relax the muscles.

- Press your tongue against the roof of your mouth. Feel the pressure at the front and back of your tongue. Relax your tongue.

- Tighten the muscles in your face, then feel them go limp.

- Raise your shoulders until your upper back feels tight. Hold the tension. Slowly lower your shoulders.

- Roll your shoulders forward a few times, then back a few

times. Bring them together, then pull them back. Release the tension.

- Take a deep breath. Slowly let it out. Feel your body relax.

- As you breathe in, tense your chest muscles. Breathe out and let them relax. Notice how tension evaporates as you breathe out.

- As you breathe in, pull your stomach in and tighten your abdominal muscles. Breathe out and let the tension go out with your breath.

- Breathe in and as you do, push your belly out to make a potbelly. Hold it. Release your breath and let your stomach return to normal. Notice how your chest relaxes with your stomach.

- Tighten your lower back muscles by slowly arching and tightening. Let them go limp and free.

- Flex your butt and thighs by pushing and arching forward. Relax.

- Tense the muscles in your feet and calves by pressing your feet downward. Feel the tension. Let your body go limp.

- Point your toes upward to tighten your shin and ankle muscles. Feel the tension in your shins, Achilles tendon, and upper foot muscles. Concentrate on the tension. Let the muscles go loose until they feel like a warm wet towel.

- Breathe in and feel your heavy lower body muscles go limp and loose as you exhale. Feel the relaxation flow and deepen.

- Feel your body go limp and loose like a soft ragdoll. Enjoy this sensation of relaxation.

Once you get into the rhythm of muscular relaxation you can add another step. As you tense the muscle, think "reee." As you loosen the muscle, think "laaaxse." The word *relax* will become conditioned to the sensation of relaxation. You might, at times, relax yourself simply by thinking the word *relax*.

You may begin to experience some control over your relaxation response after the first try or within a few weeks of daily practice.

THE MEDITATION TECHNIQUE

First find a peaceful place. Sit comfortably and repeat a single-syllable word such as *one* in silent thought over a ten-minute period. Breathe in and slowly exhale. As you breathe in, think "oooooo" in a sort of humming tone. As you exhale, extend this to "ooonnnneee." Continue the humming sound until you have finished—about 10 to 15 seconds. Then repeat the cycle for ten minutes.

Plan to do this exercise twice a day at two designated times over the next few weeks. Early morning and late afternoon may work best.

You may find that it is difficult to concentrate on the word *one* without your mind drifting to other thoughts. If your mind drifts, go back to repeating *one* when you notice that your attention has wandered. Don't try to force the other thoughts out of your awareness. Your only task during this time is to repeat the word.

THE MENTAL RELAXATION TECHNIQUE

You can relax by using your imagination. If you can create mental images, you may find this relaxation technique appealing. The following guided imagery approach is my version of the Weitzman/Davison technique. Find a peaceful place and make yourself comfortable. Try to see each of the images that the following questions suggest. Allow yourself about a minute for each image. Don't concern yourself with how well you are doing. Let the result be your answer.

- Can you imagine a yellow kite floating high in the bright blue sky?

- Can you see a dark red rose move gently in a light breeze?

- Can you picture the sight and sounds of a narrow woodland brook running under the boughs of dark green trees?

- Can you see yourself reclining restfully in a rocking chair in a quiet room?

- Is it possible for you to imagine an aquarium with brightly colored tropical fish swimming about?

- Can you imagine your body feeling like a limp ragdoll?

- Is it possible to imagine the dew quietly vaporizing from a green summer meadow?

- Can you imagine an orange autumn leaf gently rocking back and forth in the air?

- Is it possible for you to imagine the word *relax* written in soft green letters?

- Is it possible to feel the sensations of inner peace?

ALTERNATE RELAXATION TECHNIQUES

There are many ways to relax. Some of us relax while reading a book by a favorite author. Watching a tropical fish swimming in a tank can have a soothing effect. Caring for plants can result in feelings of efficacy and tranquillity. Watching birds come to a feeder or bath can promote a feeling of well-being. Find a tranquil place; sit at the center of a domed room or on a rock overlooking a lake; go to the ocean and watch the waves roll in. You also can relax through controlled breathing. Slowly take a deep breath and exhale naturally. Repeat this every ten seconds for two minutes.

Exercise promotes stress tolerance. A regular exercise program also can promote a sense of self-efficacy and self-confidence. Planned exercise trains your body to deal with stress. As a byproduct, you may find that your heartrate and blood pressure will go down as your immune system strengthens against disease and your concentration improves. Even moderate exercise—four days a week for 30 minutes a session—often makes a difference in how you handle stress.

Yet another technique is to handle one stress at a time. One stress does not have to build on the back of another. How you handle each stressor determines if you will experience d-stress or p-stress. As far as possible, deal with each stress event as it occurs to avoid a d-stress overload.

THE ACTION TECHNIQUE

Relaxation can set the stage for focused action. Next time you face a challenge—starting a project, managing a conflict, planning a course of action—put yourself into a relaxed state using one of the methods you've mastered. You are now ready to spring into action.

To mobilize for action, think of four phrases that represent a peak performance in your life—where you did the best you could. You can remember success in sports, a time when you presented your ideas clearly, or when you sang at a concert—anything where you were well satisfied with your performance.

Keep your phrases describing that time to between four and six words. Sequence them so they represent the process you followed: what happened first, second, and so forth. Here is an example:

1. I am feeling light and confident.

2. I feel a growing sense of confidence.

3. My thoughts and feelings are one.

4. I express myself with clarity.

Some experts say that you need to repeat this sequence four times. However, because we are remarkably diverse creatures and no one change method is universally effective, it may take more or less than four repetitions for you to feel mobilized.

Repeat your personal set of phrases after you finish relaxing. Practice at home—or in a quiet place to get your body, emotions, and mind geared and focused. Then practice in simulated conditions similar to where you will use this process. Soon enough you'll find out whether this technique works for you.

Step 3: Find Allies

You can develop your relaxation resources on your own. You might also want the help of a friend. If you go this route, pick someone with a soothing voice. Find a friend who will work with you at least three times a week until you master the art of relaxation. In turn, you can provide the same service for your partner.

Step 4: Seek Rewards

Your rewards can come in at least two varieties. The first is the satisfaction of mastering relaxation. It's fun to feel relaxed and know you can evoke this feeling at will. The second is the confidence that you have prepared for expected and unexpected everyday stresses.

Step 5: Measure Your Progress

Your measures can include:

- Pleasant tingling sensations in your fingers and toes
- A mind that is relatively free from intrusive anxious thoughts
- A growing sense of confidence that you can manage stress
- Fewer colds and stress sensations
- A general feeling of well-being

Now build your own Five-Point Change Program to mobilize your p-stress resources.

1. What is your direction?
2. What are your plans?
3. Who are your allies?
4. What are your rewards?
5. How is your progress measured?

POSTSCRIPT

However much you would like to, you can't avoid stress in a world of changing conditions. Inevitably, you will repeatedly face d-stress, p-stress, or both. Your chances for keeping cool in stress situations increase when you have a clear mind, a relaxed body, and a vision of what you want to accomplish. Relaxation is one p-stress method that can help you keep your mind clear and focused. You can develop considerable resistance to d-stress and disease if you combine these stress-management techniques and strategies with physical health strategies (e.g., exercise and balanced diet) and psychological health strategies (e.g., developing clear thinking and problem-solving skills).

11

Deception Detection

Join me as we enter the wily world of deception. We will examine ways to discover people who deserve your confidence and to expose those who don't. *Through developing your deception-detection skills, you can avoid changes that deceivers want you to make and get on with making the changes that benefit you.*

When you strip the mask from the face of deceit, you are less likely to be the victim of a con! More importantly, deception-detection skills give you an important way to discover people with integrity. In this process, you will find that it normally feels better to trust than to be suspicious, and that when you work with people with integrity, you don't have to watch your back. Moreover, as you broaden your confidence and assert your will for truth, people develop confidence in your word.

Deception, like change, is another of those omnibus terms with many shades of meaning. It has a pejorative connotation. Not all deceptions, however, have tragic results. To begin, let's look at everyday deceptions, humorous deceptions, and beneficial deceptions. Next we'll probe the shadowy, slippery world of exploitive deceivers. You will see why *the word of a habitual deceiver has no value.* Then we'll apply the Five-Point Change Program to building your deception-detection skills.

EVERYDAY DECEPTIONS

Everyday deceptions are common among chimpanzees, monkeys, and apes, where they "fake each other out" for food, fun, and advantage. Humans also live in a world filled with deceptions. You hear and see hundreds every day. Most are expected: The automobile company dresses up a new product so it appeals to your fantasies. The politician promises your community whatever it takes to get elected.

Research shows that deceptive behaviors average 4.3 actions per week per person and 25 lies per day per person. Most are trifling. A friend gives a humdrum excuse for arriving a few minutes late. Your neighbor brags about her son's great intellect, and you know the kid just flunked social studies. Others are mildly aggravating. An acquaintance flatters and pressures you to buy a raffle ticket that you don't want. A neighbor promises to return your punch bowl and then doesn't. Though undesirable, such pretenses do not often rise to the level of a serious problem.

Many of our deceptions are not intentional lies. Psychologist Elizabeth Loftus (1993) points out that some of our memories are false. That doesn't mean that when we relate altered memories we are calculated liars. New information interacts with recollections that interact with suggestion. The recollections we describe may reflect our creative interpretations. However, because we have the ability to distort doesn't mean that much of what we report is unreal or inaccurate.

Slanting or distorting truth can represent a clash between truth and sparing another's feelings. A friend buys an outfit that you think is ugly. You might make a neutral comment, such as "That fits you very well." Of course, you could present your opinion in a brutally *honest* but tactless way: "Wow, you have lousy taste. You should hire a style consultant!" Such comments often provoke contention and bad feelings, so you avoid the temptation.

You may mistake some people's selfish actions for intentional deceptions calculated to disadvantage you. However, most people will act in their own interest with no intention to cause you harm. Thus, they may exaggerate their capabilities if they are trying to get a job that you also desire, or disparage you to a person in whom you both have a romantic interest.

Deception is a fact of life—even among those who consider themselves to be honest people. Thus, you may occasionally invent excuses to avoid responsibility, understate conditions, or exaggerate for emphasis. In other cases, you might color reality to give yourself the benefit of the doubt. You may wheedle information by asking indirect questions. You may make assumptions about people and come to conclusions based on speculations and misinformation.

HUMOROUS DECEPTIONS

Some deceptions are intended to be humorous. Jokes fall into this category. Joe Pygmalion grew up in a family who believed they were the greatest on earth. At his elementary school's Olympic Days, Joe raced his fellow third-graders and won. He went on to win the Champion Runner Award for all of Hawthorne Grammar. Excited by his sweep of the event, he rushed to the principal and asked, "Do you think I won because I am a Pygmalion?" The principal paused, then said, "Joe, perhaps that is so. More likely you won because you are seventeen years old."

Comedy, harmless pranks, and magicians' tricks contain deceptions we find humorous or entertaining. Supermarket tabloids also are notorious for reporting improbable events, some of which are ridiculously funny: "Two-Headed Boy Eats Dinosaur Eggs for Breakfast. Desperate Mother Searches for New Supplies." According to a tabloid report by Jack Alexander in *World*, a terrorizing four-hour battle occurred between a slightly built werewolf and Southend, England, police. The werewolf allegedly "hurled cops through the air like toothpicks." Was this a case of lycanthropy, a rare disorder where the person thinks he is a wolf? Well, the four-hour battle with a snarling creature with clawlike hands might be a tad exaggerated. Still, to add to our amusement, Jack Alexander included a werewolf-detection test so you could tell if your neighbor was a werewolf. The test included checking to see if his urine was purple. That would be an interesting feat!

BENEFICIAL DECEPTIONS

Some deceptions reflect wisdom. We use them to uncover truth. King Solomon once had to decide which of two women was the real mother of a child that both claimed. To settle the dispute he drew his sword and said he would cut the child in two and give half to each woman. One woman wept and said, "Give the child to the other." Solomon thought he knew the mother from the deceiver. However, what if the deceiver had had a surge of conscience and, to save face, blurted, "Give the child to the other," before the real mother could speak?

Trickery can preserve life. For example, what would you think of a kidnap victim who deceived her captors to escape? What of the blowfish that fools the predator into thinking that it is too big a mouthful?

In war, the military uses trickery to achieve victory by causing the enemy to misread the numbers and power of its forces. Genghis Kahn caused his enemies to think he led a massive horde, and many foes ran rather than face what was actually a much smaller force. In the present day, we call such deceptions "disinformation." This form of strategic lying is the idea behind the axiom that truth is the first casualty of war. Here the military's goal is to mislead the enemy by camouflaging, decoying, shading, adjusting, and laundering information to gain advantage.

If you play poker, you want your opponent to think you have greater or lesser strength in your hand than you actually do. Successful bluffs make it likely that your competitor will err in your favor.

If you run a company and want to keep a new product secret, you probably will use creative deceptions to hide information from your competition. But if you mislead the public by saying that your company's dividend is safe just before you eliminate it, then you have stepped into the world of exploitive deception.

EXPLOITIVE DECEPTIONS

It is the rare person who doesn't take some deceptive initiatives. Most of us tell white lies or slant the truth to spare others from embarrassment, to avoid difficult confrontations, to preserve peace and harmony, to cloak feelings of inferiority, to avoid punishment, or to gain status. Still, some deceptions may cause the deceiver a loss of credibility and your confidence. A friend who openly lies to you may not long remain a friend. The type of lie, who initiates it, and what it means to you will determine your response.

Deceptions come in many costly ways. A bank robber *innocently* tells the arresting officer he really wasn't trying to rob the bank; someone put the gun in his hand. Ex-U.S. Senator Harrison Williams took a bribe from an FBI agent posing as an Arab sheik. Then, when he saw the videotape of the transaction, he said the money was not a bribe; it was a campaign contribution. A contractor uses cheap materials, overcharges you, and skips town. An auto mechanic punches a hole in your muffler, then sells you an expensive exhaust system. You win a few games from a cardsharp before you get cleaned out. Your faithless lover says you are the one and then spends a weekend in bed with your best friend.

Exploitive deceivers profit by misleading you and robbing you of something you value. They may cost you time, money, status, love, or peace of mind—possibly your life. They have a secret: You will believe what you want to hear. That simple concept is their key to your pocketbook, heart, or life. They'll tell you anything to gain advantage. They play by their rules and not the conventional ones you are accustomed to following.

Exploitive deceptions put you at an unfair disadvantage. If you see clearly how exploitive deceivers operate, you can avoid many tricks that could hook and harm you. The most common type of deceiver you should be alert to is the parasitic helper.

Parasitic helpers may be huckstering lawyers promising to turn your minor injury into a big payoff. They may be Bible-thumping ministers promising you spiritual solace if you send $20 to their mailing address. They may be "financial advisers" promising amazing returns on a small investment, or "doctors" touting miracle cures for untreatable diseases. They may be the used-car salesperson who says, "Trust me, I'm on your side." They may be cosmeticians who tell you they can stop your skin from aging. They can be self-proclaimed "counselors" who tell you they can cure all your mental ills. They can be financial predators out to steal your life savings through confidence games.

What do all members of this deceiver community have in common? They purport to want to help you out of the goodness of their hearts. What is the invariable result? They give you words; you give them money, sex, or power.

Sex, money, power, and greed motivate people to deceive other people. What motivates you to believe their lies? There are numerous reasons: (1) You want to hear that whatever you desire is *easily* within your grasp. (2) You want to free yourself from an affliction that you want to believe the con artist can cure. (3) You don't want to lose out on the "opportunity of a lifetime." (4) You want the con artist's approval, so you hesitate to challenge the pitch for fear of earning disapproval. (5) You think it is easier to go along rather than risk a confrontation by raising hard questions. (6) You trust the apparent logic of the sales pitch over your own judgment. (7) You don't want to think that a person who takes the time to develop a relationship with you can take advantage of the relationship.

These are some of the conditions that the deliberate deceivers count on. They don't want you to walk away. They'll tell you whatever it takes to hook you. They prefer trusting, vulnerable people or those with big egos whom they can manipulate. They like people who expect fairness and will bend over to give others the benefit of the doubt. Remember, deceivers don't play by conventional rules. They count on your playing by those rules and not taking the steps to disbelieve.

Deceivers also have recognizable reactions when exposed. Intimidation, coercion, and bullying are the final line of defense for a deceiver—especially a public figure such as a politician, professional, or businessperson caught in a scandal. So once you have exposed a pathological deceiver, expect to hear arrogant denials. Expect that this person will gloss over the facts and appeal to emotional issues. Expect Machiavellian manipulation where political expediency rises above morality. Remember: You can always walk away or fight back if you are otherwise sure to be harmed.

BUILDING DECEPTION-DETECTION SKILLS

Statistics are another common form of deception. For example, research over the past 50 years has consistently shown that about 80 percent of the population will lie or cheat if they think they can get away with it. Yet, you will find considerable individual differences in types and frequencies of deceptive acts. Some people rarely deceive. For others, deception is a way of life. The deception statistics demonstrate that you will have many opportunities to practice your deception-detection skills. Let's see how to apply the Five-Point Change Program to deception detection.

Step 1: Set a Direction

We find our direction for deception detection when we seek truth. Thus, this mission is to separate truth from deceit in order to improve the quality of our judgments. To start, let's look at the meaning of truth.

Truth can be relative. It also changes as our knowledge grows. A truth: A tiger runs faster than a zebra. But suppose we learn more: Some zebras run faster than some tigers. Our knowledge about the truth of the relative speed of animal life has evolved. So we know that truth can involve variance and can never be an exact reality. Still, a true statement, as in "You're not likely to escape a tiger by riding away on a zebra," carries a high degree of certainty if not a high degree of probability of occurrence. In contrast, "We all die" is a statement with a very high certainty *and* probability.

Undoubtedly there are different degrees of truth. For example, a used-car salesperson may truthfully tell you that an elderly teacher once owned the car you want. What this person doesn't tell you is that the car was a lemon from the moment it rolled off the production line in Detroit, and that is why the teacher dumped it.

When I say two plus two equals four, I am mathematically correct. Yet, although two apples plus two apples equals four apples, the first two apples may weigh more than the second two. So they are not equal in weight. The same holds for the idea that two quarters plus two quarters equals four quarters. The first two quarters may be 1918 Philadelphia-minted silver Standing Liberty quarters in MS-65 condition. The other two may be bag-marked 1984 copper-alloy coins. The difference in value may be thousands of dollars. The quarters are not equivalent in value although they are equal in number.

Therefore, when I say "I believe this is true," I am giving you my honest perception. I'm telling you the truth, but I could be wrong.

Truth sometimes blends with our impressions. Suppose we say

"Judy is more attractive than Susan." If Judy looks like a Miss America candidate and Susan suffers from anorexia nervosa, we may have a consensus. Still, in many matters of taste and aesthetics, truth is fuzzy and may not exist at all!

If our Five-Point Program's mission is to seek truth, we must prepare ourselves to acknowledge many gray areas of truth. Still, our truth-seeking goals would best include the acquisition of facts and a faithful report of the reality that we see.

Step 2: Make Plans

You can't always trust your feelings—remember that irrational ideas feel real. But if you don't feel right about something, perhaps there is a reason.

In this deception-detection plan, we'll look at ways to uncover exploitive deceptions that can cause you emotional, physical, or economic harm. We'll use deception clues to load the dice in your favor. These clues are like flashing yellow lights—they urge caution by signaling potential danger. They are not infallible. Even if they were, we are not infallible observers and thinkers!

Part of your plan would be to look out for these clues:

- Be alert to vague but impressive statements, deliberate silences, double-talk, and the inactive tense to obfuscate responsibility.

- Use facts to separate your wishes from reality. For example, when you try to arrange a lunch with someone who keeps politely putting you off and offers encouraging excuses such as "I'd really love to, but my cousin is coming to town," don't take false hope in the words. Look at the results.

- Watch for incongruities. Is something said or done too often, too emphatically, or in a strange way? For example, a husband frequently told his wife how disgusted he was with the infidelities of his married male co-workers. One day she picked up a credit card statement and saw that he was booking motel rooms all over the city. His virtuous posturing had been a smoke screen for his philandering. She saw, in hindsight, that he had protested far too often and too vigorously.

- Watch for inconsistencies. Prolific liars are likely to contradict themselves because they forget all the lies they've told. Lawyers and investigators will often ask the same question more than once because liars often forget what they just said.

- Avoid the consensus trap. If you listen to a conservative radio talk show, you will get a consensus from the participants that is likely to differ from the consensus on a talk show hosted by a liberal. People with common views usually gather and agree on the same bias. Get the facts before you make up your mind.

- Beware the myth that deceivers can't look you in the eye. There is some evidence that some deceivers will look you in the eye longer than people speaking the truth. Some honest and shy persons will look away from you because they feel self-conscious.

- Be alert to people who use indefinite passive tense phrases such as "The program was ineffective" or "It was decided that the dog would run free." They are often trying to obscure the lines of responsibility.

- Beware of arguments with emotional issues attached. For example, Iraq's leader Saddam Hussein tied his withdrawal from Kuwait to the emotional Arab–Israeli conflict issue. That issue was not related to the invasion.

- Don't be too quick to judge people on appearance. We are less likely to view attractive-looking people as deceivers. Look for disparities between style and substance. Ask yourself: Do this person's thoughts sound logical and reasonable? How can I check the information? Then check it.

- Watch out for character assassins. Some deceivers will sidetrack issues by casting doubt in your mind about someone else's character, actions, or intentions.

- Beware of people who claim to speak or act "for your own good." For example, if a colleague tells you that you probably shouldn't apply for a promotion because management will soon eliminate the job, you might want to learn if the colleague or the colleague's friend wants the job.

- Be on the alert for people who try to pull a fast one. Take note when someone tries to brush past your interests so fast you cannot respond in time to protect yourself. If you feel rushed, ask who benefits, in what way do they benefit, and at whose cost? If possible, delay all decisions until you can study the situation.

- Be on the lookout for convenient memory lapses. The deceiver often conceals information by pretending to forget. If the person's memory seems sharp and intact about most other matters, suspect deception and probe further.

- Listen to what is missing. Deceivers will often hold back information. Job applicants who say they believe in teamwork and describe their accomplishments without crediting others may lack teamwork skills.

- Look for differences between words and body language. Is the verbal message consistent with the person's tone and body language? People with pasted-on smiles whose body language suggests stress—perhaps anger—are concealing their real feelings and motives.

- Be alert to the dishonest defense. When you find an unscrupulous businessperson, administrator, professional, tradesperson, or neighbor, don't expect the deceiver to act honestly after you've uncovered and exposed the lie. He or she will try harder next time—if there is a next time!

Deception-detection clues are useful but fallible indicators. You can use them to decide whether you must gather more information about a person or condition that can threaten your important self-interests.

The bum deal awareness technique, plausibility technique, and relationship-building strategy are tools for evaluating different dubious situations, and can help you maintain clarity of thought and perspective.

THE BUM DEAL AWARENESS TECHNIQUE

This technique will help you avoid con artists. Apply the following clues before you commit your money or resources:

- Watch out for the deal that is too good to be true. Get-rich-quick-without-risk schemes are grounds for suspicion. For example, if someone offers you a 30 percent return on your money each year, watch out! Unless we have a 25 percent inflation rate, chances are the deal is a scam.

- Ask yourself why an acquaintance would want to let you in on a fabulous million-dollar opportunity. What makes you special? If you have any doubts, back off.

- Watch out for people who say, "Trust me." Judge people's trustworthiness by their actions, not their words. Get a history with the person before committing your funds and resources to his or her cause.

- Look behind the words to see what they represent. Smoothly delivered words such as *wonderful, fabulous, amazing, astonishing,* and *revolutionary* can refocus our attention from the salient issues. Carefully examine any highly optimistic worded proposition. Get beyond the words and get to the facts.

- If a person sounds too polished and rehearsed, suspect deception.

THE PLAUSIBILITY TECHNIQUE

Crooks don't necessarily look like crooks. Some practiced liars sound confident, sincere, and honest even when they are knowingly defrauding you. Most people are persuaded by this display of confidence and don't look beyond surface cues.

Most practiced deceivers sound and act the same whether they tell lies or tell the truth. Indeed, some scoundrels don't trust the truth even when it is their best defense. That is where this plausibility technique can help you distinguish friend from scoundrel.

You can ask these questions to test a statement's validity:

- Does the statement sound plausible?

- Is the statement verifiable?

- Is it congruous with experience?

- Is it consistent with known facts?

- What would I gain by believing or disbelieving this statement?

- Would knowledgeable people agree with this statement?

- What are the probable motives behind the statement?

Also watch body posturing. Deceivers, when challenged, will often show a restricted range of body movements. They look poised, but don't be fooled.

THE RELATIONSHIP-BUILDING STRATEGY

It is a rare person who has never been fooled in love. Some studies say that 50 percent of all married men and about 30 percent of all married women have cheated on their mates at least once. There are many examples of false lovers who tell their temporary adored that they are the one and only at the same time they are planning to marry or run off with someone else.

How do you find out if your lover is cheating on you? There are many clues. An unusual pattern of business meetings and out-of-town conferences may cause you to raise your eyebrows. You call late and no one answers. This happens again and again. Credit card bills show a change in routine that now includes a pattern of luncheon and motel expenses on the same day. Exaggerated reassurances, withdrawal, unusually long shopping trips—all promote suspicion. A straightforward question, "What's going on?" can help you to start to put these matters into perspective.

Because love is such an intense emotion and trust is so important to binding a stable future with someone, a third degree is *not* the best way to forge a healthy relationship. Rather, take an entirely different perspective and circumvent these problems by building authenticity into your relationship. This strategy has four parts:

1. Most of us believe that what we want is reasonable. In some cases this leads to a reform school atmosphere where one thinks he or she needs to train the other to comply. *What is reasonable may not be realistic!* Asking what is "both reasonable and realistic" can help you focus on an achievable goal and eliminate the conflicts between desires and reality that lead to deceptions. For example, you may not get your introverted mate to enjoy parties, but you can more readily accomplish a compromise where you set aside a total of eight hours each month when you go to the movies together with friends, have dinner out, go roller skating—anything that allows for social interaction.

2. The second part pivots on two words: *common cause.* Couples who have a common cause to which both feel committed—writing books, building a business, gardening, raising children, evolving their relationship—have a basis for making compromises. Trade-offs and letting the other win (sometimes) can serve two purposes: They help you build quality into your relationship and provide a reason to put aside bickering in the service of a greater good.

3. The third part involves *announcing.* Honest explanations can defuse unnecessary contention. When you are feeling irritated, depressed, blameful, or negative, let your mate know. That way the other won't feel angry, responsible, or guilty—all emotions that can kindle a fire of deception. When you are honest about your changes, your mate may show greater tolerance than if your actions went without explanation.

4. The fourth part involves *timing* and *pacing.* We all are subject to irritating moods, have some problem habits, and don't always think with a straight head. Sometimes we need to talk out these matters so that we can change and do better. The question is, how much can you say, and when? Timing is particularly important because you are less likely

to be reactionary and escalate a conflict when you choose the best time to have a dispassionate discussion.

The four parts of the relationship-building technique can help you shrink the frequency of unnecessary arguments and reduce the risk that your lover will be disloyal and deceptive. But suppose you have a deceptive lover in your life, and you don't feel comfortable about exercising this technique (or the timing isn't right, or you feel too angry)? You have many alternatives: (1) Have a talk with your lover in which you can say, without being possessive, that any further breaches of trust will cause you to seriously think of ending the relationship. (2) Accept an unfortunate situation and make the best of it (not a particularly good alternative, but sometimes a rational choice). (3) Effect a trial separation—a cooling-off period where you can both put your relationship into perspective and see if it is worth continuing. (4) Break up the relationship and get on with your life. This last change normally is warranted when you can clearly see that the relationship will be over sooner or later. Perhaps the change is better made sooner than later.

I know it is extremely difficult to face deception in a primary relationship. Our emotions often are intense, we may not think clearly, and there is a lot at stake. I can say that if you are clear and specific on the changes you want in your relationship and if those changes are reasonable, you will feel more in control of yourself than people who know only that they just want change.

LIMITATIONS TO DECEPTION-DETECTION TECHNIQUES

While you are still in your planning stage, it is important to note that going too far in deception detection can be dangerous. The techniques just discussed can help you to distinguish friends from misguided deceivers and to recognize exploitive deceivers. However, there is a caveat: It is risky to read too much into situations. Keep these ideas in mind:

- Many well-meaning people misspeak their thoughts and thus might appear deceptive when they are not. We also misinterpret because of gaps in our knowledge and personal bias—the deception detector also self-deceives!

- Many people bias their interpretations of events because they believe they should be on a certain side of an issue. In expecting a compelling wish to be right, they unconsciously exclude disconfirming information.

Most people will show inaccuracies in their perceptions. At some time or another, most people will make mistakes in what they say—because they are human, or because they have been misinformed, or because they lack certain information. They have no desire to deceive.

The art of deception detection is to maintain a fluid view of the changing set of circumstances, a healthy skepticism, and a willingness to confront ambiguous issues and still be able to tolerate other people's foibles and faults.

Step 3: Find Allies

Deception-detection methods help you discover trustworthy people with integrity. As this group grows around you, you will have more people resources to draw upon in your truth-seeking efforts. Here are a few people who can help:

- Some of your allies may be researchers or investigators who study problems that interest you and who can be counted on to present objective findings.

- People who have an interest in getting to the truth will support similar efforts on your part.

- Professional counselors, with no vested interests, can prove helpful when the truth you seek concerns the validity of your attitudes and beliefs. They can serve as a sounding board and help you define your perspectives.

Step 4: Seek Rewards

The most obvious reward of successful deception detection is that you avoid having someone gyp or mislead you. Specifically, that means:

- Slick operators will fool you less often. Thus, your choices will be more directly in your interests.

- When you routinely separate fact from deception, you can put your time and resources to wiser use.

- Your investments will be safer.

- You will purchase more of what you need and less of what others want to sell you.

Your most satisfying rewards will come when you identify people who have integrity and deserve your trust and support.

Step 5: Measure Your Progress

You can measure your deception-detection progress by asking yourself these questions. Do you:

- Have fewer complications and more challenges?

- Maintain a healthy skepticism for deals that sound too good to be true?

- Use deception-detection methods to discover whom you can trust?

- Effectively use the bum deal technique, plausibility technique, and relationship-building strategy when appropriate?

It is now your turn to design a Five-Point Change Program for building your deception-detection skills.

1. What is your direction?

2. What are your plans?

3. Who are your allies?

4. What are your rewards?

5. How do you measure your progress?

POSTSCRIPT

Normally, you do better when you are authentic and sensitive in your communications with yourself and equitable and honest in dealing with others. You'll have a clearer head. You'll feel more confident in your *self*. Your personal and intimate relations will be more heavily marked by trust.

In striving for this ideal, you can't realistically cast all deceptions into the same basket. Deceptions come in different types, and truth appears in different shades of gray. The deceptions you initiate and those you squarely face will depend on the situation, the power of the receiver or deceiver, and the quality of your judgment. However, there are three generalizations that rise above the rest: (1) Trust grows from honesty. (2) Positive self-development is a byproduct of adapting your resources to meet changing challenges forthrightly. (3) How you progress, in large measure, depends on your perception of truth.

12

Working Changes

We commonly hear statements such as these about our work life:

- We spend most of our waking hours in work.

- The average person makes four career changes.

- Job satisfaction ranks high as an important goal.

- Most people report they don't get enough satisfaction from their work.

What does all this mean? Simply that it makes sense to work at a career that pleases you.

When you give people the choice of inactivity or work, most prefer to make an effort to accomplish something. The alternative is mental and physical vegetation.

Sensory-deprivation studies show that when experimenters deprive paid volunteer subjects of sensory input for a few days, they become disoriented, hallucinate, panic, feel nauseated, and perform poorly on intelligence tests. They soon quit this "job" despite extraordinarily high pay for doing nothing! The subjects' reactions, admittedly under abnormal conditions, demonstrate that when we don't have meaningful activity, we lose equilibrium.

WHAT WORKS FOR YOU?

People like to do what they can do well. You excel when you concentrate on what is profitable, where you have talent, and where you work hard at what comes easiest. This is the secret of the rapid-fire money producers: the top entertainers, competent managers, world-class athletes, and others. People from these select groups earn money in proportion to the value other people place on their skills.

To think like a rapid money producer, ask yourself, "Where can I make the most dollars in the most enjoyable way?" Consider:

- What are your highest dollar-producing resources?
- What is the market for these skills and talents?
- What is the entry fee?
- Are you willing to pay the price?
- What can you expect in return for your efforts?

There is another dimension to developing a satisfying career. People who work hard at "what comes easy" are tough to beat. But few find such high levels of work satisfaction that vacations become unwelcome interruptions. However, why not shoot for the ideal? Even if you don't get your dream job, you might come enjoyably close.

YOUR CAREER ANALYSIS

A career self-analysis is a valuable undertaking for those who want to add to their work satisfaction.

You can move closer to your ideal job by first profiling your interests and capabilities and then comparing them with available job opportunities. In your personal profile, you define what you consider purposeful work, the work functions you prefer, your strongest abilities, your work values, your dispositions, and the work level that most closely fits your skills and capabilities.

Developing this career profile serves a triple purpose: (1) You clarify the type of meaningful work you want to accomplish, (2) you match the results of your analysis against a potential job opportunity, and (3) you look for opportunities on your present job where you can routinely apply your skills and interests. With that in mind, ask yourself these six questions about job satisfaction. You may want to write down your answers.

1. *What do you consider purposeful and productive work?* People who work at jobs they view as purposeful and productive experience a sense of fulfillment and have an abundance of career satisfaction. To begin, start with your most recent job and work back toward when you were in school. What work efforts gave you the most satisfaction? Next, group these functions into general categories such as helping people, solving problems, or following through.

2. *What are your preferred work functions?* Work involves different tasks. Some activities we enjoy; others we find unpleasant, even stressful. People who find satisfaction in their work perform more operations that they find productive. Job operations include a broad spectrum of different activities, including writing a report, making a sales call, tilling a field, researching a problem, or devising a plan. List the work functions you have enjoyed most.

3. *What are your strongest abilities?* Effective people feel a sense of achievement in areas in which they are most competent. Do you have an aptitude for math? Do you have a knack for dealing with people? Do you have a skill you enjoy developing?

4. *What are your work values?* Do you persist until you finish? Do you value producing a quality product? Do you value conscientiousness? Do you value loyalty? Do you see yourself as acting responsibly even at a personal cost?

5. *What are your prime work dispositions and qualities?* Consider career directions that fit your disposition. If you are

energetic and competitive, you may feel stressed working at a job that requires you to behave in a subdued and deferent manner. If you have a sensitive temperament, you may experience stress working in an environment where you deal with contentious people. If you prefer to work by yourself, you may feel stressed if your job requires that you work with and through others.

6. *At what occupational level do you operate most effectively?* When you test your abilities, you discover how far you can stretch. If you stretch too far, you may go beyond what you can do effectively. For instance, you may have exceptional talent in sales but not work well as a sales manager because each role involves different functions. However, you may have to try out the job to discover your limitations. If you don't stretch far enough, you'll have fewer accomplishments and frustrate yourself.

As you go through this exercise, you may find that your answers to these questions overlap. This overlap could be significant. Consider it highlighted information, from which you may develop a generalization that describes your prime career direction. For instance, you might discover that your best career path involves providing subordinate managers with opportunities to develop their aptitudes and abilities through their work.

BUILDING U-INC.

Your career analysis is a tool to help you predict where you can get the most work satisfaction. This knowledge is the backdrop for career opportunities.

To add velocity to your career-satisfaction program, pretend you are a company called U-Incorporated and use that model to organize your efforts. U-Inc. is your company; you can make it responsive to whatever you wish, from an environmental problem to a political cause. Your imaginary U-Inc. is a fun way to structure your career efforts along with the Five-Point Change Program.

Step 1: Find a Direction

Profitable companies have a clear direction; a supporting business plan; and strategies to develop, promote, and sell their products. To succeed, management organizes its resources and concentrates on what the company does best. Xerox produces copy equipment, not broomsticks. H&R Block provides tax assistance, not janitorial services.

At U-Inc., you are the product and "you" includes your talents, skills, and other constructive attributes. The purpose of U-Inc. is to organize your career resources to concentrate on what you do best.

U-Inc. has a basic mission: to develop your talents, to advance your career interests, and to enjoy the process. This mission is consistent with any constructive activity, including writing a column for a newspaper by using rhymes to describe the humor of our times.

Step 2: Make Plans

Companies have chief executive officers (CEOs) who are responsible for organizing and coordinating the efforts of their organization. They also have proprietary control systems to support their efforts. At U-Inc., you are the top brass! You create the proprietary control system. Here are some ways you can achieve your mission:

- Experiment with new ways to do your work. By breaking from your usual routine, you can learn what works and what doesn't work.

- Look at how other people perform the same functions you do. What can you adapt to your work situation?

- Make your career a cause. Your cause can be a dedication to quality, innovativeness, effectiveness, human relations, problem solving, or whatever you choose.

- Volunteer for causes that complement your career. What you learn from helping out for a worthy cause can expand your work skills and capabilities.

Naturally, you'd like to have your plan work. Not only do you want to learn about your career resources and have fun doing so, but you want to profit from your efforts. You will face snags on any career path, and you must make revisions if you want to progress. You may want an acting career, but after several years, you haven't landed any roles. Still, you can explore alternate routes. Perhaps you can find a new way to achieve your ambition; perhaps you must abandon this quest and accept acting as an avocational interest.

THE DEPARTMENT TECHNIQUE

In designing U-Inc., you can invent *departments* to support your ideal job description. Departmentalizing is a vital element of your proprietary control system.

Think about developing an imaginary marketing department. Your marketing efforts will help you learn what the market wants and what you have to offer that fits. Your talents and skills are like products. When you look at the markets you want to enter, see how your ideal job description fits those markets. Then put your marketing efforts into selectively targeting your efforts where people appreciate your talents.

You can create new departments at any time. A strategic planning department looks at the long term. Where are you going to be 3, 5, 10, and 20 years from now?

Step 3: Find Allies

Companies have boards of directors. You, too, can have a board to advise and counsel you. You can pick the board members from among your family, friends, and associates. Your board members will normally look at your career plans and actions with sensitivity and impartiality. You can bounce ideas off various board members.

You can make your board informal and call upon each separately if you wish. You also can convene a formal board. Consider the advantages of convening a formal board quarterly to review your career progress. You might get some exceptional ideas when people brainstorm about U-Inc.

Have your board review your goals, plans, and progress. Like helpful allies, they can suggest challenging new courses to chart. Still, as CEO, you reserve the right to decide how U-Inc. will operate.

Step 4: Seek Rewards

What do you get out of developing U-Inc. resources? You will experience one or more of the following:

- Competency
- Emotional freedom
- Enthusiasm
- Confidence
- Playfulness
- A sense of accomplishment

Step 5: Measure Your Progress

You can measure your career achievements against the "Four C's of Progress." Do you routinely,

- Commit yourself to follow a growth pathway?
- Challenge yourself to discover what you can do?
- Command your abilities and talents?
- Compete in a tough world?

If you can say yes to at least two C's of Progress, you are on a constructive career path.

Let's get to work and develop U-Inc. Write your own Five-Point Program to help you achieve your goals.

1. What is your direction?

2. What are your plans?

3. Who are your allies?

4. What are your rewards?

5. How do you measure your progress?

POSTSCRIPT

You, the U-Inc. entrepreneur, choose your career path and forge constructive changes others only dream of making. Since your product is you, you decide what your job enrichment goals are, how to build your talents, and when and where to act. As a byproduct, you may feel a growing sense of competency, increased work confidence, and the satisfaction that comes from constructively absorbing yourself in what you do.

By developing yourself through your work, you may find out more about your likes, drives, and capabilities than you might now anticipate.

Sigmund Freud said that the essence of life is love and work. I extend this idea to include: If you enjoy your work, you are likely to take greater pleasure in your life.

Part Three

Roadblocks to Change and How to Avoid Them

13

Banishing Illusions and Self-Deceptions

After reading Part Two, you may rightly feel optimistic about your ability to create change. What, then, if you soon find yourself spinning your wheels and going nowhere fast? How does this happen? What can you now do to power the changes that you believe you can make?

Plans rarely run smoothly. The unexpected happens. Outside events will affect the direction and speed of your change efforts. More often, you may unintentionally impede your constructive changing. In this phase of your journey, we'll look at how illusions fog reality, mental traps keep you running in circles, classic roadblocks cause unnecessary detours, and procrastination keeps you waiting by the side of the road.

First we'll deal with harmful illusions. In this chapter I will first describe techniques for uncovering illusions that weigh you down and then suggest ways to drop them from your mind. You'll learn how to recognize the snares and pitfalls of illusions that make your change elusive.

WHAT ARE ILLUSIONS?

Illusions are false impressions, misconceptions, or delusions. Like the air, they are there. Some you recognize; some you don't. Some are fun. Some are curative. Some are deadly.

Illusions can be fun. We consciously suspend our skepticism for the sake of amusement. We enjoy watching Mickey Mouse although we know he is the product of a cartoonist's pen. The moon appears to move as we walk. The magician David Copperfield makes a locomotive disappear before our eyes. We see illusions in the mirages that rise from desert sands where towering cities shimmer in the sun and waters glimmer on the horizon. As we approach, the mirages vanish like puffs of steam.

Some illusions can even act like medication. Psychologist Lauren Alloy (1992) notes that people who believe they have control over events in their lives are less likely to feel depressed. She describes this belief as the optimistic illusion—mental health link.

The optimistic mental health link can actually cause beneficial changes in your body chemistry. For example, a strong belief that you have control over a metastasizing cancer—where you imagine your white corpuscles moving like the characters in a video game, gobbling up cancer cells—can result in reduced distress. With less distress, chances are that your body will produce less of the immune system—suppressing hormone cortisol. A strong immune system gives you more of a fighting chance against disease.

Illusions give structure to life to make it understandable. Sometimes they serve a useful purpose. Your best friend dies in an accident and you hear it is "meant to be." You have terminal cancer and believe a cure is around the corner. In other cases, illusions divert attention from problems. You blame your failures on your history.

Our major illusions help explain our states of uncertainty, provide simple answers to seemingly unfathomable questions, support what we want to believe, explain our feelings, dull our awareness of an unpleasant reality, and sweeten a sour situation.

Illusions reduce uncertainty and threat. Since threat is likely to occur during the formative stages of any significant change, we are inclined to delude ourselves into thinking that we need to resist the change and maintain the status quo.

Illusions have other characteristics:

- Illusions explain away misery, although they may bring more misery in the long run. The suffering wife of an alcoholic refuses to take charge of her life. Instead, she excuses her husband's drunken behavior by saying he only drinks because his job is stressful. She cushions her upset with the false hope that he will change when his job improves. She refuses to admit to herself that his job won't improve as long as he drinks. She is imprisoned in circular logic: She is helpless until her husband quits drinking, and as long as he keeps drinking, she is helpless.

- Illusions reflect different states of mind. When two people have an emotionally charged disagreement, they may have different opinions on the sequence of events and their motives. Yet both think they are correct.

- Illusions make life glow. In a state of romantic love, people see no faults in their lover — only awe-inspiring qualities. However, once past the illusionary phase, many lovers begin to see faults in their partners, or see them in a different light.

- Illusions dull our awareness of reality. A man, after several divorces, says he was very devoted to each of his wives. He cannot understand why his marriages ended. But the consequences of his actions tell the real story.

Some illusions are euphemisms. For example: Hitler called the extermination of millions of Jews, "the final solution." Thus, he created the illusion that this mass killing was merely a solution to a problem.

Other illusions are linked to the culture. In a society that worships youth, growing old is feared. Like Ponce de León, we search for the fountain of youth; only now, we hope to find it in a cold cream jar or a surgeon's scalpel. Some people arrest their mental states. In their thirties and forties, they see themselves as college-age youths in a vain attempt to cast aside the bleak reality of aging.

Where Illusions Come From

We are very inventive creatures. We have the power to develop unusual myths and create strange beliefs. Some of these are dangerously self-deceptive. If you believe that your reflexes improve after a few drinks, you may misjudge your ability to drive an automobile while under the influence. Gamblers who believe that Lady Luck will allow them to defy the laws of chance and come out winners eventually lose more than they win. And the desperate people who look for magical remedies to tough problems wait in vain for solutions.

Because we are suggestible creatures, we can absorb illusions from outside sources. Your family, friends, and teachers expose you to their illusions. You may come to believe that only people with your religious, economic, or educational background are good people. As a teen you may dress and act like your peers because you want to belong to a group. You may identify with an organization and faithfully accept any of the myths the leadership supports.

We tend to be most receptive to viewpoints that fit with our prejudices. Edward Epstein (1989) reports that Lenin created an illusion for American business that he (Lenin) thought that communism was a failure. He used industrialist Armond Hammer to convince businesspeople that investing in the Soviet Union was both prudent and safe. Since most American businesspersons believed in capitalism, they were easy to convince. But it was all an illusion, as history showed. Communism continued in the Soviet Union for another 65 years. The investments produced few profits.

Self-Deceptive Illusions

Many of us organize our lives around illusions. They can propel action as muscles power movement.

Some of the most common illusions are those of insight, judgment, identity, inferiority, superiority, and success. Recognizing and overcoming these self-deceptions is critical if you are to think with a clearer head and move forward on the path of change.

THE ILLUSION OF INSIGHT

When under an illusion of insight, your intuition dominates. You decide about people's character based on first impressions and never suspect that you could be wrong. You base your decision on how you feel at the time.

Let's take an extreme example. A paranoid, who believes that the FBI has a surveillance team watching him, may base this belief on haphazard events. He hears rustling leaves and sees shadows when he walks. He solidly believes his mental apparitions are true because they explain why he feels so strange inside. He doesn't recognize the fallacy in his circular reasoning which flows around this logic: The FBI is watching me; I know this because I feel observed; I feel observed because the FBI watches me. When he points to haphazard events to justify the feeling, he exposes a second fallacious mental loop: The FBI is there because the leaves are rustling; the leaves are rustling because the FBI is there. He hangs onto this persecution perception (also called a restitution symptom) as though his psychic life depended on its continuance. Although his insight clashes with outside reality, he sees no inconsistency because he has deceived himself.

THE ILLUSION OF JUDGMENT

The illusion of judgment is the belief that our judgments are invariably valid. A supervisor, for example, may reject a subordinate's well-thought-out suggestion because she believes she is consistently right and therefore her subordinate must be wrong.

The illusion of judgment is harmful when it stimulates you to repeat the same mistakes or become enmeshed in recurrent crises. Examples: You accept a job because of the title, but your skills lie elsewhere. You involve yourself in intimate relationships with people who exploit your good will. You underevaluate your skills and get less for your efforts.

It is hard to deal effectively with reality when the illusion of judgment shapes your perceptions. Still, if you know what clues to look for in order to detect this illusion, you won't be so quick to deceive yourself.

To measure the quality of your judgment, create a percentage scale. Keep a record of your judgments and their results. Are you correct 100 percent, 90 percent, or 10 percent of the time? How did you verify the correctness of your judgments? What does your correctness index tell you about the accuracy of your judgments?

Admittedly, keeping a box score on your judgments is tough to do. However, if you spot check yourself from time to time, you may discover some patterns and trends that help indicate whether your decisions are shaped by illusionary conjecture or by vision, reason, and fact.

The illusion of judgment is like an iron thread that weaves through other illusion systems. See if you can recognize it in the illusions of identity, inferiority, superiority, and success.

THE ILLUSION OF IDENTITY

People who derive their self-worth from identifying with their families, organizations, automobiles, clothing, or neighborhoods act as if their affiliations and possessions define their inner worth. This illusion—that inner worth and outside achievement are the same— is widespread, particularly in competitive industrial societies. Here we foolishly make our human worth depend upon what we do, our family origin, and other questionable measures.

Illusions of identity stick like glue. When people base their worth on a group affiliation, symbol, object, or ideal, they will resist new ideas and struggle to defend the illusion because the illusion tells them who they are.

Joining an organization or group that you believe reflects your interests, values, and beliefs is generally positive. But you stretch the point when you come to believe your personal worth comes from that affiliation.

Clearly, the solution to this problem is to ground your identity more to your inner self than to a job, a mate, a house, a car, or a reference group. That is easily said but not so easily accomplished. The power of an illusion of identity is such that we bind ourselves to an outside entity or set of beliefs, even when we have an intellectual understanding of the folly of this false identification.

THE ILLUSION OF INFERIORITY

Cartoonist Walt Kelly's Pogo said, "We have met the enemy and he is us." Our opossum friend implied that, more than anything or anyone else, *we* block our ability to enjoy successful and happy lives.

The feeling of inferiority is a common illusion. When pressed by this illusion, even the smallest changes look out of reach. Author and dock worker Eric Hoffer (1952) recognized this human fault when he remarked that self-loathing leads to a crisis in self-esteem, and that this feeling engulfs us when we face the unknown and fear the new.

The illusion of inferiority rarely comes in pure form. Typically there are as many different complications as there are different people who feel inferior. Ted's case illustrates a common version:

When I first saw Ted he impressed me as a bright, impeccably groomed, deferent person who tried very hard to be friendly. Once I got beyond his polished appearance, however, I saw a different picture.

Ted had many painful symptoms. He worried about personal disaster. Would his wife divorce him? Would he get fired? Would his neighbor sue him? Would lightning strike him? He repeated the rhetorical question, Will I get through the day? The question is rhetorical because there is an implied answer—I cannot!

He also tended to sink into obsessive fits fueled by a fear of making a mistake. He continually questioned himself. Did he turn on his telephone answering machine? Did he lock the door? Did he remember to pack his report in his briefcase?

Ted was haunted by his obsessive thoughts and befuddled by his compulsive activities. He worried about his image and whether he looked good. So he spent about an hour in the shower each morning. He felt foolish and out of control but believed he couldn't stop himself. He grabbed for snacks when he felt tense, then hated himself when he looked in the mirror and saw his gut hanging over his belt buckle. He feared that unless he got control over his eating, he would die young.

What happened here? Ted had a proclivity toward this obsessive-compulsive pattern and engaged in these activities when he felt tense. He didn't trust himself. Those two issues were the crux of his problem.

Ted was able to change slowly, in stages. He emerged from the illusion trap first by recognizing that his notions of inferiority smothered his admirable attributes. Then, he learned that he could cope with most daily challenges if he allowed himself to live through his tensions. By repeatedly showing himself that he had worthwhile qualities, he weakened the pull of these distracting symptoms. Although not completely free of his illusion of inferiority, Ted now can perceive of himself as a person with valuable resources who can make progress.

Most of us have resources we can develop within the limitations set by nature. So none of us are inferior beings—even those of us who obsess their way through a day!

THE ILLUSION OF SUPERIORITY

People who suffer from the illusion of superiority overestimate their capabilities. In a milder form of this illusion, they give themselves the benefit of the doubt. At the extreme, they lionize their attributes and unwaveringly believe their subjective judgments are valid.

Most of us suffer from the superiority illusion to a greater or lesser degree. If such an individual, for instance, couldn't find his car keys, he might ask, "Honey, what did you do with my car keys?" or "Why don't those kids leave my stuff alone?" He wouldn't think of saying, "Darn, I misplaced my keys again. I'd better retrace my steps."

Psychologist James Sully's (1884) classic study revealed that people seriously afflicted with the illusion of superiority suffer from a distorted self-image. Often they are constructing a defense against hidden inferiority feelings.

The illusion of superiority has some short-term advantages. For example, the deluded person might plunge into areas that others would not try. Still, poor results often follow. Suppose a weak administrator applies for a higher-level job. If she is overconfident, she will fool herself and may fool the decision maker into believing she'll succeed at a higher level. Only later will they both discover that she was not prepared for the job.

THE ILLUSIONS BEHIND THE FEAR OF SUCCESS

Fear of success often grows from the illusion that achievement leads to failure. Here people fear success because they lack the confidence that they can stay successful. They also may fear that others will expect much more of them than they can deliver.

This is the falling-star version of the fear of failure syndrome. The fretful and terrorized person expects to tumble from the lofty perch and so doesn't want to rise too high. Success also feels threatening to people who think they don't deserve it, because success violates their derogatory self-concepts.

Sam has a fear of success. He says that if he is successful, he will lose his wife's love and affection, since she is very supportive when he has setbacks. He fears she will abandon him if he does better.

Sam's fear of success grows from the belief that success carries unpleasant results. There are other dimensions to this fear. Sam doesn't believe he will have the energy to keep up the pace that "success" requires. He believes that he will face higher demands that he cannot meet.

This man lacks evidence to support his fear about losing his wife's love and support. Indeed, when I met his wife, I found her a naturally supportive person. She wanted him to succeed. She would support his successes and support him if he did not accomplish what he set out to do.

Sam has a long list of excellent qualities, traits, and skills. But he discounts those qualities and focuses his attention instead on his deficiencies, imperfections, and fears. He believes his wife stays with him only because he "is" a failure.

Sam's fear is based on the belief that he doesn't deserve to succeed. He believes the irrational idea because the idea feels real and he has never examined it closely. Thus, he also suffers from the twin illusions of insight and judgment.

Once exposed, his illusions gradually weakened. Enlightenment began when Sam saw that success was relative. I pointed out, for example, that although he worked below his potential, he could pay his mortgage, accumulate modest savings, and remain unencumbered by unpaid bills. He grudgingly admitted that his financial condition represented a certain degree of success. The illusion further weakened when he considered that if he had reached this level of success and none of his dire predictions had come true, he had no reason to think that a gradual increase in income would figuratively bring his house down on top of him. The illusion was battered again when he admitted that his wife was bright and practical. Why would a bright, practical person marry him if he had little to offer her? Sam forced himself to clarify and then reconcile these two incompatible ideas, and this effort gradually gave him a different perspective and one less set of restrictive illusions.

Freedom from the Illusion Trap

We are creatures of change who can think about our thinking, recognize patterns and trends in our behavior, and learn to adapt and change. If you have blind spots (illusions) and don't see them, where do you begin to change? Here is an important clue: *You can recognize illusions by their results.*

When the same unfortunate things happen to you, chances are an illusion is behind the turmoil. So, look particularly hard if you've had several failed marriages, feel stifled in your career, or cannot get started on your program of change. Look for a pattern of unwanted feelings such as emotional distress, or problem habits such as gambling, smoking, or procrastination. Look at the gaps in your life—what you want to accomplish, and can accomplish, but avoid. Sometimes seeing what is missing in your life opens the blinds to discovering an illusion that interferes with the purposeful changes you would normally choose to make.

Follow these five steps to identify and eliminate self-defeating illusions:

1. Keep a daily diary.

2. Record events where you got poor results.

3. Review your diary at monthly intervals and look for recurring patterns of thought and belief connected to those unfortunate results.

4. Examine how your actions may have caused the outcome.

5. Work to change the thinking and actions that contributed to the pattern, and see if the results change.

This process can lead to the type of personal satisfaction that comes from knowing you have an important set of illusion-detection tools you can use to cut through distortions to get to the facts and the truth. You will have an objective basis for making decisions and thus feeling more confident in your judgments. You also will feel the sense of control that comes when you believe you can change a pattern you could not understand or change before.

This illusion-breaking process is not as simple as it may first appear. Even when you learn to recognize your most self-defeating illusion, you will have difficulty letting go of it. The power of an illusion lies in its continuing to dominate your perspective even when you know you are deceiving yourself. Don't blame yourself, just keep trying. The struggle is worth it.

POSTSCRIPT

Illusions range from fun to neutral to harmful. Some produce mixed results.

Illusion detection is productive and can be fun. As you identify and cut through self-defeating illusions, you add muscle to your fact-based belief system and are more likely to organize your efforts around sound beliefs. When you rid yourself of harmful illusions, you experience a growing sense of confidence as a change maker.

People who shed unproductive and false illusions don't become cynical or callous. They have more creative energy and time to enjoy their friends and their lives.

14

Winning the Struggle Within

Our most heroic struggles occur within ourselves. On this battleground, titanic clashes arise between our wish to grow and irrational processes that slow or stop this progression. To put the struggle into focus, let's see how our inner gremlins—who feed these irrational processes—can be confronted by our rational minds. You can learn to recognize and challenge gremlin tricks, gain self-knowledge, and add to your change-making skills.

THE GREMLINS INSIDE US

Gremlins are, by nature, nefarious creatures. They gleefully test our wits by confusing our minds with mental pollutants (called superstitions and false hopes) and mental pitfalls. They like to trap us and keep us in the trap. It's in their nature.

As we enter the scene, we see the gremlin busily pouring mind-altering ingredients into three different cauldrons. Then as the fires build beneath these pots, green, red, and yellow ooze begins to bubble furiously. The wily gremlin cackles with delight as it beholds this glowing sight.

It knows three things. The green brew makes people vulnerable to superstition. The red brings false hopes. The yellow clouds judgment and reason. When the brews are ready, the gremlin uses them to distract humans' minds.

Fortunately, your rational perspective can resist the effects of the brew. It takes more effort to maintain your rational perspective than to brew your own gremlin potions, but I think you'll find the struggle worth the trouble.

Superstitious Thinking

In its first assault, the gremlin aerates the world with a green mist to cause people to think superstitiously. Soon the minds of people are clattering with strange thoughts, such as "Cross your fingers, close your eyes, say hallelujah twice, and you will be safe from harm."

The gremlin knows that we are very susceptible to superstition. "People," it muses, "will do almost anything to feel protected against the unknown, to control future events, and to feel safe and secure. I will simply spread the word that there are magical ways to ensure good fortune, to ward off disaster, and to draw energy from the universe or from crystals for healing.

"The brew fills people's minds with false hopes. They avoid stepping on cracks to avoid breaking Mother's back. They don't walk under ladders. They are careful not to break mirrors. They believe that bad things come in threes. They get anxious each time a Friday the thirteenth arrives. What a gas!"

THE RATIONAL RESPONSE

We are rarely far from our roots when we think superstitiously. The ancient Greeks invented Olympic gods to explain phenomena they did not understand. We invented astrology, palm reading, and tarot cards in the feeble hope that we could gain knowledge to control an unclear future. It's a farce. If today's horoscope said that you would meet a swarthy stranger, imagine millions of people with the same reading meeting swarthy strangers at the same time. This superstitious thinking does nothing to improve the quality of our lives. Nevertheless, we fertilize these beliefs despite evidence that they are baseless.

These magical beliefs reflect our desire to have a way to protect our health and security. Superstitions give us a false sense of control. For example, you might cross your fingers for luck to avoid misfortune. Unfortunately, crossing your fingers cannot control an outcome already in motion. This is about as effective as twisting your body and flinging out your arms to make a bowling ball veer in one direction or another after the ball has left your hand.

Superstitious people distort reality through circular logic. After Bram Stoker wrote his story of Dracula, our ancestors used garlic to ward off humanoid vampires. This is a classic example of circular logic. You wear garlic and no vampire attacks you. Because you don't get bitten, you think the garlic protected you. Yet people who don't wear garlic also don't get bitten by vampires because there are no such vampires around to bite them.

Superstitions take four major forms:

1. *Superstitions that promise to protect against illness.* In the seventeenth century, people believed that eating mummy flesh was a remedy for illness. In the eighteenth century some people believed that if they ate while a funeral bell tolled, they would get a toothache.

2. *Superstitions that promise luck.* Some people believe that the right hand is lucky and the left unlucky. Folks carry a rabbit's foot or fasten horseshoes over doors for good luck. Some athletes continue to wear the same socks during their sports season as long as they continue to do well.

3. *Superstitions that promise protective covenant.* Satanic cult members perform ritual sacrifices to gain the favor of a mythical devil. To avoid bad luck, we refuse to walk under ladders or break mirrors or to allow a black cat to cross our path. (In the British Isles, a black cat is good luck!)

4. *Superstitions that promise eternal youth.* When we believe we can look and feel young by having electronic facial massages,

we enter the world of superstition. People who go through this process don't change in appearance. They just *think* they look younger. Remember Ponce de León and his search for the fountain of youth?

As we understand reality better, we rely less and less on magical ways of knowing and more upon our rational resources.

False Hopes

The gremlin uses the red brew to pollute the world's waters with the false hope of four happiness contingencies. Here is the gremlin's message: "It is every human's birthright to be successful, approved of, in control, and comfortable. With this come love, wealth, serenity, and health without strings or conditions. Meet these contingencies and be genuinely happy." Does this idea sound appealing? Think again.

THE RATIONAL RESPONSE

We are easy marks for gremlin logic when we believe we deserve to be happy and that we can count on good things in life appearing like a rabbit out of a magician's hat. Although the idea sounds appealing, its consequences are not. We can't ever meet these contingencies because they are false goals. We cannot achieve them without risk and action any more than we can expect fairy godmothers to make us glamorous or a philosopher's stone to make us wise. Nevertheless, these irrational expectations often lead to frustrated and anguished feelings. The contingencies are false goals because they are abstract. Happiness and success in the real world happen only through focused concrete actions such as facing a challenge.

Let's look closer at the destructive power of false hopes.

1. *The need for success* leads to intense, pressured, perfectionistic striving to reach an ideal. This frantic struggle causes reality distortions, a narrow perspective, intolerance, and misdirected drive. Your rational perspective can expose irrational assumptions beneath these common beliefs:

- My worth depends on my performance.

- A failing grade means I am a failure.

- Everything I do should be perfect.

- I must succeed in whatever I do.

Success as its own aim is an abstract goal. If you enter this mindframe, whatever success you have will not be enough. It is better to concentrate on making excellent performances. It is then that you discover the meaning of inner power.

2. *The need for approval* often leads to a nonassertive fawning style. Your rational perspective can expose the irrational assumptions that underlie this fake need:

- People should treat me with respect.

- It would be horrible if anyone rejected me.

- I must not say, do, or think anything that would cause others to think badly of me.

- People should applaud me no matter what I do.

To counter this gremlin trick, ask yourself if you would trade something valuable for the approval of another. Would you give up your health, your reason, or your life?

3. *The need for control* leads to phobic reactions, manipulative behavior, compulsions, hostility, defensiveness, stiffness, and self-concept disorders. Control is not the problem. Humans have a natural tendency to control their environment. It is the misplaced *need* for control that causes trouble. Your rational mind can expose the irrational assumptions that underlie this need for control:

- People should do what I expect of them.

- I should never look or act weak.

- I must grasp all that I hear and read.

- I must have guarantees.

We all live in a whirlpool of changing conditions. In this living maelstrom, you often have imperfect information and imperfect skills to meet unclear challenges. Sometimes the best you can do is the best you can do.

4. *The need for comfort* leads to procrastination, impulsive decisions, avoidance, and addictive habits such as smoking, gambling, and compulsive eating. Your rational mind can expose the irrational assumptions that underlie the need for comfort:

- I can't stand what I don't like.

- It's awful when I don't get what I want when I want it.

- My life should be easier.

- If I ignore my problems, they will disappear.

Frantic attempts to feel good or comfortable often have paradoxical effects. People who insist on feeling good often feel tense. They go for short-term goals. Although most of us prefer to feel comfortable and secure, there is no natural law that guarantees that we have a perfect right to perpetual bliss. We can develop our environment to lift the probability that we will feel secure, but there are no guarantees.

Most people will lead tragic lives because they get the gremlin's message, accept what they hear, and never think there is an alternative way to view life. This one-way thinking puts them into a box, makes them easily frustrated, and brings chronic feelings of insecurity and instability. If you get caught in the gremlin trap of false hopes, you have nowhere to go.

The gremlin's false hopes lead to self-imprisonment when we make our happiness depend on achieving an unrealistic Utopia. Thus, when we insist that we will settle for nothing less than absolute happiness, respect, satisfaction, wealth, love, success, or self-esteem, we incarcerate ourselves in prisons of our own design.

These demands and idealistic expectations are the mortar that holds together our prisons of false hopes. Reality awareness is the key to the prison gate. Reflective thought is required to find the key and to discover how to use it.

Eight Traps of Judgment and Thinking

The gremlin sprayed the deadly yellow brew everywhere to cloud judgment and reason, and so led people into eight erroneous thinking traps. Let's see how we can expose the irrationality behind the allure of these traps.

TRAP 1: ALLNESS THINKING

The gremlin tells us, "Your neighbors are all skunks and rats. Never trust them. They will cheat you whenever they have the chance."

When you fall into the allness-thinking trap, you make vague statements that mean very little. Allness thinking includes *always* and *never* ideas. General, all-encompassing statements are examples of careless thinking. We use them when we want to assassinate people's characters or choose not to address the facts.

The problem with allness thinking is that it is self-limiting. When you use vague statements to express yourself, you fog your communications and obscure your problems.

To escape the trap, get specific with yourself. Look for exceptions. There is no need to buy into generalizations when you have access to the descriptive facts.

TRAP 2: ABSOLUTE DEMANDS

The gremlin urges, "You should get what you expect. If you expect that your mate should cater to your every wish, it should be the way you want."

This is the absolute-demand trap; there is no flexibility behind the bars of this prison. When your wishes and wants become expectations and demands, you turn life into a living hell. Demands include pressuring ideas such as *should, ought to,* and *must.* These one-way insistences are symptoms of fear and inflexibility. People upset themselves when they demand a reality that cannot be. You cannot expect your mate to cater to your every wish. People will not always do what you want. These expectations lead to exasperation.

Watch out for the disguised demand like the innocent-sounding question: "Why do these things always happen to me?" The real message often is, "These things should not happen to me."

When you feel upset, look for a *should, ought to,* or *must* in your thoughts. Psychoanalyst Karen Horney (1950) calls them tyrannical because they are irrational claims that you and others can't fulfill. But not all *shoulds* are that way. Brittle, rigid, and unyielding *shoulds* differ radically from the benign, conditional *shoulds* that simply suggest a course of action: "I should remind myself to pick up bread after work."

To help free yourself from the pain of these demands, substitute *preferences* for *irrational shoulds.* "I *prefer* it this way" has a much more rational ring than "It *should* be my way."

TRAP 3: INTOLERANT ABSTRACTIONS

The gremlin laughs as it presents a selection of vague but distressing thoughts. It teaches that "it is a horror for you to feel inconvenienced. You should not have any awful experiences." It knows that intolerant abstractions turn your inner world into a bundle of knots. That is because intolerant terms often evoke strong stress emotions that cloud the rational chambers of your mind. They include vague and overused words such as *awful, terrible,* and *horrible.* If you want to explore this trap, ask yourself what *horrible* actually means.

You can break loose when you get rid of demands and vague abstractions, and forthrightly express your likes and dislikes: "I feel pleased with the result" or "I felt displeased when I heard the news." If the situation warrants stronger language, why not use more descriptive ideas such as *tragic, distressing,* or *highly inconvenient?*

TRAP 4: THE "IS" OF IDENTITY

Now for a favorite gremlin trick: using the verb *to be* to create fuzzy thinking and cause emotional havoc. Used effectively, gremlins know that this verb colors a person's sense of identity. Here are two samples of incorrect "to be" thinking: "I *am* no good" and "you *are* worthless." Here the chances to assassinate people's character are endless. The gremlin muses, "All you have to say is that Sam *is* a thief and many people will believe Sam is a thief."

The "is" of identity distorts reality by oversimplifying a complex person. For example, when I say "I *am* great," I make a false statement about myself. When I say "I *am* rotten," I falsely condemn myself. The bottom line: Character generalizations, expressed by the verb *to be*, distort reality.

With practice, you can substitute objective statements for identity statements. For example, instead of declaring yourself rotten, you can be specific: "I *acted* poorly when I forgot to bid farewell to my host." By focusing on specific behaviors, you have given yourself something to change. However, when you say you *are* "bad," what can you do?

Our emotions are a very important sign of the type of thinking that is going on in our heads. So if you feel an acute anxiety, depression, guilt, or inferiority, look for the "is" of identity.

TRAP 5: THE ALL-INCLUSIVE TRAP

The gremlin also uses an innocent pronoun, "it," to obfuscate reality. Like the "is" of identity, vague pronouns such as *it* often disguise issues and allow us to block ourselves from seeing reality. The gremlin advises us to express our ideas equivocally. Statements such as "It stinks" are the gremlin's favorites because you don't have to "think out" your thinking.

Watch for this all-inclusive trap. It contains two jagged teeth: The unclear reference and the ambiguous pronoun. When I say "I hate *it*," "it" has many possible meanings. Can you tell what "it" means? Just as when I say *"Everybody* dislikes Tom," I'm sure we could find exceptions. This ambiguous pronoun "everybody" does not represent a universe of thought about Tom.

We can easily stress ourselves when we use unclear referents. For example, the statement "I can't stand it" represents an ambiguous and stressful state of mind. What is the "it" you can't stand? Is "it" your anxiety?

We respond rationally when we make the statement specific and verifiable. For example, saying "I dislike it when my boss criticizes my work in front of my co-workers" is significantly less stressful than saying "I hate work" or "Life stinks." Why? Because when you get specific about what makes you feel uncomfortable, you can realistically look for ways to work on the problem.

TRAP 6: THE GENERALIZATION TRAP

Generalizations can be quite accurate. The generalization that grasshoppers don't hear certain tones is accurate, as is the generalization that women normally have better fine motor coordination than men.

Not all generalizations reflect reality, though. The gremlin leaps in glee at the thought that it can persuade people to generalize from exceptional examples. The possibilities are endless. If Joe the politician takes a bribe, then all politicians are crooks. If Sandy tells one lie, you can never again believe what Sandy says. Overgeneralizing this way gives you a false feeling of comfort.

People sometimes fall into the generalization trap because of limited experience. A young man who gets turned down by two women in succession may believe that no one will want to date him. So he may withdraw or make half-hearted future efforts that only tend to support the prophecy.

TRAP 7: THE DICHOTOMY TRAP

The gremlin supports the "is" of identity and generalization traps when it uses false dichotomies. By encouraging you to classify people according to narrow categories of *good* and *bad* or *noble* and *ignoble*, it seeks to limit your perspective. The statements "John is a good man" and "Sandra is a bad person" show the limitations to this thinking.

Your rational mind tells you that gremlin dichotomies are false. People are like rainbows in that they have many colors and sides to their personalities. People do not just have either–or, and black–white attributes. Instead, they have and–also characteristics.

TRAP 8: THE CAUSE AND EFFECT TRAP

The gremlin clouds our minds with illogical thoughts, such as "If your friend cancels a dinner with you, it must mean the friend despises you." This reasoning assumes that there can be only one cause for an unwanted action.

We fall into the gremlin's cause-and-effect trap when we believe that single causes explain complex human events. There are many ways to reframe problems: If your mate does not come home at an appointed time, does that mean he or she is having an affair? Or does it perhaps mean that your spouse had to remain at a meeting and there was no phone available on which to call you? To stay out of the cause-and-effect trap, ask yourself these questions: If you removed the presumed cause, would the outcome change? If the cause changed, would your outlook change? If there were multiple causes, would that change your perspective?

Some events have several causes. Let's say, for example, that an egg falls to the floor and breaks. Does that mean that the shell is weak, the egg landed on the wrong side, it fell too great a distance, or it landed on too hard a surface?

We fall into the cause-and-effect trap when we confuse correlation with cause. For example, a child's teeth will come in before the child learns to walk. Does that mean the growth of teeth causes the walking? We call such illogical inferences a non sequitur, which means "it doesn't follow." In most cases, this kind of reasoning doesn't make sense. For example, people who feel distressed and tell themselves they have no friends simply because they made a mistake fall into the cause-and-effect trap.

A cause for a one-time event—missing your bus once—is different from the causes for a pattern—missing the bus two days every week. You have to look closely at the meaning and mechanisms of the pattern if you wish to break from the cause-and-effect trap.

We have other ways to escape the trap. We can, for instance, think using multiple perspectives. That is, we can experience and assimilate many ideas about the same person, idea, or event. We also can see consistency and exceptions. With a developed pluralistic view of life, you can cross-check your viewpoint by examining an event from different perspectives.

Monolithic thinking (the idea that there is only one possible explanation) can get us into emotional jams. Multiple perspective thinking can get us out. Let's get back to the gremlin's example. A friend agrees to have dinner with you. Then, at the last minute, she cancels without explanation. Do you assume she doesn't want to have dinner with you because she really doesn't like you? Think about another possibility. Yes, she does want to have dinner with you, but an emergency came up that was more important than having fun with you. Now, check out your hypothesis. Get more information. That is how to think using plausible multiple perspectives.

When you use multiple perspective thinking strategies, you get away from the rigid black-or-white thinking of the pessimist and the optimist and you view life from the perspective of an omnimist—that is my word for one who sees shadings, degrees, and variances. This ability to think using multiple perspectives enables you to orchestrate experience. You also are more likely to recognize the truth when you see it.

POSTSCRIPT

During turbulent times, we are especially susceptible to superstition, false hopes, and misconceptions for guidance. We tend to look to powers outside of ourselves to grant us the security we can achieve on our own.

You can use your rational mind to combat these "powers" by breaking them down, analyzing them, and exposing them to the light of the truth.

15

Beating the Classic Change Blockers

Have you ever wanted to make a change, seen the benefits clearly, known what to do, then felt stymied because you kept sidetracking yourself? Illusions and myths can inhibit change, but they are not the only impediments. Indeed, they are often accompanied by blockers. So to sharpen your awareness of these blockers, I'll tell you about some that feel so normal that you don't ordinarily pay attention to them. Nevertheless, they drastically freeze your choices, limit your opportunities, and cause you to repeat mistakes.

WHAT'S YOUR BLOCK?

The snake said to the frog, "Come with me, my friend, and I will help you find paradise." The frog joined the snake and disappeared.

Why do many smart people think and act like frogs? Why do they follow patterns that repeatedly cause them harm? Why do they resist changes that will help them? Perhaps the better questions to ask are: How do people go about blocking themselves from making purposeful changes? What are the critical change blockers that can sidetrack you on your journey of change?

To put this matter into perspective, think about a habit you want to break—something you want to *stop* doing: snacking on potato chips, smoking, or bickering with your mate. Next, think about the advantages of breaking the habit. Then promise yourself you will stop. As you make the promise, do you feel some resistance building up inside of you? If so, listen to your inner voice. Are you telling yourself something like "I'll quit tomorrow" or "I can't do it" or "I'm sure I'll fail"? Now, think about something you put off that you want to do: taking a course to develop computer skills, learning to speak before groups, or making five new sales contacts each week. Promise yourself you'll take action and follow through starting now. Now, listen to yourself. Are you sending a conflicting message, such as "I don't have the time right now," "I don't think I will succeed," or "I'll do it when I feel motivated"? If you hear yourself thinking this way, you have tuned into your inner voice of resistance.

Psychologist Michael Mahoney (1991) has identified five main theories that explain why people resist change: motivational avoidance, motivational deficit, ambivalence, reactance, and self-protection. Let's look at each and determine which make the most sense.

Motivation Avoidance

Mahoney describes Sigmund Freud, the founder of psychoanalysis, as a pessimistic *motivation-avoidance* theorist. Freud saw people as clinging to their pathologies due to childhood conflicts and unconsciously motivated drives. Mahoney notes that Freud viewed resistance as a self-defeating dynamism. He goes on to say that contrary to Freud's views, resistance sometimes serves functional purposes such as helping a person preserve his or her sense of organization, balance, and functionality.

Aside from this difference in opinion, there is another matter that stretches the credulity of the psychoanalytic system of change. Analysts frequently use circular historical theories to explain current behavior. Suppose you believed an analytic interpretation that people who grovel for affection do so because they were affectively starved as children, and they have repressed and denied this awareness. That interpretation carries these risks: (1) Each condition explains the other and, because of that, cannot be proven; (2) such circular connections are often proven false under scientific tests; (3) the foundation assumptions can, and often do, prove faulty; and (4) it is unlikely that all people who grovel for affection do so for identical reasons. Mahoney's position on psychoanalysis invites this conclusion: If you use questionable explanatory tools you may not get to the root of the real problems. You can understand, therefore, why Mahoney thinks that motivation-avoidance theories are problematical.

Motivation Deficit

People exhibiting this pattern presumably lack sufficient drive or reinforcement to change. Mahoney rightly points out that motivational-deficit theories are too simplistic to explain complex human behavior. They largely have been discredited because they also rely on an illogical circularity: You don't change because you are not motivated; you don't have the right motivation, and that is why you don't change. The definitions for motivation, reinforcement, and change are connected. Each defines, relies on, and explains the other.

Ambivalence

Mahoney thinks better of the theory of *ambivalence* of choice, which says that people are paralyzed because they want to do two opposite and incompatible things. For example, you eat chocolate bars because you have chocolate urges and the candy tastes good; yet you gain weight when you eat chocolate, and you want to trim down. The typical choice is between short-term satisfaction (eating the chocolate) and long-term advantage (losing weight and staying trim). Short-term satisfaction, such as eating chocolate bars, can prove tough to resist. But sometimes you can resolve your ambivalence by embracing an equivalent but saner choice: You substitute cocoa (which contains less fat per ounce) or carob for chocolate.

Reactance

This is a term sociologists borrowed from the physical sciences. Reactance describes a process of resistance that follows when you *perceive* that you are forced to change an activity you once had the freedom to perform. Plantation owners resisted the abolition of slavery, and the Civil War was fought by the South partially to reverse this change. Rum running and drinking at speakeasies was common during Prohibition. Today, smokers in the "smoke-free" workplace may rebel by taking excessive time smoking outside.

Self-Protection

This is when you have a healthy concern about the outcome of a change because it may jeopardize important ways that you organize your thoughts or do things. Here you have an investment in the system. Examples: You choose not to buy into a get-rich scheme because you want to keep your life's savings. You want to continue using the same theory of psychology because you invested time and money in the process. You opt not to divorce your ill-tempered mate because you prefer to continue living in your mansion and divorce would force the sale of your home.

The ambivalence, reactance, and self-protective theories better explain resistance to change because they seem consistent with everyday observations of how people actually think and behave.

Because ambivalence, reactance, and self-protection often operate in concert with each other, it is important to know *how* they interact. It is also useful to know that this combination can signal a sensible emotional resistance that prompts you to avoid unhealthy changes.

Consider, for example, a woman who feels ambivalent about starting a relationship with a man she believes may not be faithful to her. She finds him intelligent, charming, and appealing and she thinks he will be instrumental in overcoming her feelings of loneliness. But she also wants a monogamous relationship, and he has said he does not intend to change his lifestyle. Further, the relationship may cause her to give up some of the things she enjoys. She loves hiking, and he thinks hiking and hikers are boring. She enjoys a nightly glass of wine, and he is a reformed alcohol abuser who preaches to her about the evils of booze. She believes that he would seek to control what she does and says; she feels protective about freedoms that she would have to give up. Thus she rightly resists the change—starting a relationship with him—because it is mostly in her self-interest to do so.

THE TEN PRIME CHANGE BLOCKERS

People resist healthy changes for many irrational reasons, and they have developed several self-protective mechanisms that needlessly restrict their flexibility. In the remainder of this chapter, we'll look at ten specific "self-protective" change blockers and discuss techniques for overcoming them. The blockers include the grouser's downfall, the turtle trap, the competition trap, the perfectionism trap, the emotional-resistance trap, the learned-helplessness trap, the fallback trap, the conflict-avoidance trap, the complacency trap, and the limitations trap. As you examine these patterns, think about whether you have fallen into any of these traps and stopped yourself from taking action to change. If so, consider what you can do to alter your thinking and behavior.

The Grouser's Downfall

Grousers are people who whine, complain, blame, and find fault. They busy themselves fingering others for causing the disasters in their lives and thus they exonerate themselves and avoid facing the real reasons for their lack of progress.

Grousers will complain about having autocratic bosses and insist that the boss's attitude prevents them from testing out innovative new ideas. They also complain that their mates hold them back. They find their children too demanding, their neighbors too inconsiderate, and service providers ungrateful and difficult.

Grousers are so focused on reasons why they can't get started that they miss the point: You decide what is relevant to do and then you *find* ways to get it done. Focusing on problems and finding solutions is a big part of the challenge of living.

Grousers are not in control of themselves. They are poor self-managers because they don't focus and concentrate their efforts on achieving their relevant goals. Therefore, they suffer from a lack of accomplishment, feel insecure, and seek new people to blame for their inability to act effectively.

If you are in this trap, there are ways out. Accept that you are responsible for what you do. And although there are going to be impediments, you'd better figure out how to work for productive results whether you get cooperation or not. There is no other reasonable way to go.

The Turtle Trap

The heart of the turtle trap is fear of change. Here you pull your head into your shell, seeking comfort in the familiar, trying hopelessly to avoid changing conditions. You want the world to stop so you have no new problems to solve.

Timothy was in the turtle trap. This lonely 45-year-old man felt overwhelmed by life and so he looked for guarantees. He stayed in his cluttered home and refused to take risks to expand his world.

When I first saw him, Timothy said he felt alienated and that he was living a miserable life. Since he was afraid that he could never successfully relate to people, I encouraged him to join a therapy group. He did, and to his credit, stayed despite many initial frustrations.

The group repeatedly worked to help him get his head out of his shell, but the harder they tried the more he withdrew. He had his first breakthrough when, unexpectedly, a shy young woman, Molly, burst into tears of frustration over his behavior. She tried hard to get through to him and felt repeatedly thwarted by his rigid *turtle* defenses. It was then that he momentarily stopped focusing on himself and his rigidity melted like a snowflake on a hot stove.

With the group's help, Timothy saw that the way he had frustrated Molly—his refusal to relate to others on an emotional level—was the same way he frustrated himself. He cried in relief when he saw that when he left his safe shell, he could feel emotional closeness.

His second insight came when he discovered that different people could reject and approve of him for the same reasons. One person might admire his clothing; another might think he had bad taste in clothing. One might think he was too distant; another might appreciate his respect for privacy.

Timothy began to become more outgoing after accepting these two rational awarenesses. Still, even highly motivated people such as Timothy require time to change. In the process, they discover that the result is not perfect and that regression is as natural as progression. Nonetheless, these undulations are better than sticking your head into a darkened shell and looking out at a bleak and narrow field of choices.

To help yourself out of this trap, reflect on your earlier dreams and aspirations that remain unaccomplished. Think about what is still possible for you to achieve. Envision going through the Five-Point Change Program to reach your goal. Imagine yourself enjoying the steps in the process.

The Competition Trap

We think of competition as vying, struggling, and winning. Even in cultures where people frown on competition, they compete on how noncompetitive they can be! Competition limits you when you feel threatened or make half-hearted efforts; in this instance, fear of competition is a change blocker. But when you set your sights beyond your opponents—to do the best you can do—then competitors only help your self-improvement efforts.

Competition is part of life. Through competition you learn where you need to improve and where your strengths give you an edge. You listen to your competitors' arguments, and you develop a counter plan that helps you stretch. You watch what your competition does, and you devise strategies to improve. Competition, then, provides incentives for self-improvement and opportunities to discover what you can do.

Consider that a competition is not just a win–lose affair. You can compete and win alongside your competitors. A contest with friends about who can lose the most weight in three months can spur you and your friends on to heights of shared achievement. Completing a marathon can make you feel a surge of accomplishment—even if you come in last. Here, meeting your objective of completing the race is more important than your ranking. You also can compete with yourself. Make a game of facing new challenges and try to exceed your prior performance.

The Perfectionism Trap

Many perfectionists feel as if they are "eating themselves up inside" over small matters—getting upset when someone leaves a dirty dish in the sink, something gets spilled on the floor, or a bed remains unmade. But perfectionism is more than nitpicking. A philosophy runs through these symptoms: I must be the best or I am nothing.

People who embrace the perfectionist's philosophy feel worthless when they fall short of their standards. They fear a loss of control and place rigid restrictions on themselves—and others—to feel safe. They believe they (and other people) should live according to their lofty expectations, and they condemn anyone who falls short of these stratospheric heights.

Perfectionists live a life of conflicting feelings. They feel inferior yet self-righteous. In the either–or world of the perfectionist, life looks black or white, good or bad, wonderful or horrible. They struggle as hard as they can, only to feel stressed to the breaking point—the opposite of what they say they want. This is the perfectionist's paradox. And when they tie their human worth to impossible goals, they discover the road to paralysis.

Because they constantly strive for what they cannot obtain, perfectionists believe they are constantly falling behind. They routinely lament over their inability to make up for lost time and opportunities. Paradoxically, perfectionists believe they are the best and others are inferior; sometimes, though, they think everybody is superior to them. Interestingly, these mind sets change with circumstances and are interspersed with periods of tolerant understanding. One evaluation rule of thumb: The shorter the periods of tolerance, the greater the perfectionistic leanings.

If after reading this you still seek perfection, pick up a lamp and follow Diogenes in your endless search for the unattainable.

The Emotional-Resistance Trap

People tend to resist changes that don't "feel right." Sometimes these emotional signals are intuitively accurate, and you can trust your basic feelings. Still, you can evaluate your "feeling judgments" better when you understand how what you are thinking and feeling fits with what is really going on around you. Some emotions come from distorted thinking and are powerful change blockers. Let's look at three emotional states that are at the heart of emotional distress and that block or delay constructive change:

- *Hostility* is a grandiose emotional state bristling with belligerence and hatred. The feeling flows from arrogant beliefs such as "Nobody should thwart me. I am all powerful. I will beat down anyone who stands in my way." When this is a life theme, the hostile person routinely goes against others.

- *Anxiety* is the fear that we cannot cope with real or imagined future events. It ranges from apprehension to terror. Anxious people immobilize themselves with "what if" thinking: What if she rejects me? What if I fail? What if I look like a fool? The anxious person has a stressful answer built into these questions—it would be horrible if I am rejected, fail, or look foolish; I am too inferior to survive the event.

- *Depression* is a bleak view of the future. Here you see yourself as mentally feeble, helpless, and hopeless. Self-pity dominates your conscious thought. At the extreme, family, friends, work, and life all seem hollow. You feel dead inside. It is at this most dismal point that a change for the better is often close.

Anxiety and depression share a common idea: "I'm helpless because I can't cope." The *can't cope* feature of anxiety promotes avoidance but sometimes evokes physical feelings of excitation, heart palpitations, shortness of breath, or dizziness. When these sensations appear, you tend to concentrate more on the tension symptoms than on the depression, and thus may not realize you also feel depressed.

The perceived sense of helplessness in depression also has a *can't cope* theme. When the dominant physical sensations are inhibition and ponderous thought, sluggish movements, and weepy feelings, these conditions may dominate the anxiety that often accompanies depression.

Sometimes hostility flows into this picture. For example, you feel angry because you feel stuck. Then you resentfully blame conditions or other people for your emotional state. When this hostility dominates over anxiety and depression, you will tend to obsess and this will often shut you off from directly experiencing your anxiety and depression. Hostility also can evoke anxiety. You feel an aggressive impulse and this frightens you. Under such conditions, you might tensely back off from even the most legitimate confrontations.

You can change this *disturbing triad* of anxiety, depression, and hostility by rationally facing your problems. Make a plan using the rational-emotive behavior strategies you learned about in Chapter 6. Execute the plan, and keep executing it, until you have established a sense of well-being.

You might also imagine that the challenge of overcoming this disturbing triad is like confronting a holographic block of ice. If you want to go through, you have to take the chance that the ice is a mirage.

The Learned-Helplessness Trap

No one knows with certainty what will happen today, tomorrow, or next year. Unexpected events can affect you whether you like it or not—one day your pet disappears or the company you work for goes bankrupt.

Most people temporarily feel helpless when faced with what they see as a drastic change. They then take steps to modify or adapt or accept the change. Some, however, depress themselves when confronted by an event they think they can't control, can't change, or can't manage. Although some events are legitimately out of reasonable control—a professional thief steals your new automobile while you sleep—others, such as obtaining a new job or rebounding after a romantic breakup, are difficulties that you can work to resolve. However, if you believe that you are too frail and vulnerable to cope with adversity and that you can't do anything about the events of life, you will avoid tackling significant problems that actually are solvable. This sense of resignation parallels a form of depression that psychologist Martin Seligman (1975) describes as *learned helplessness*.

You feel helpless when you believe you can't assert independent control over your life. When combined with feelings of depression, this attitude takes over your mind. You forget that you have learned much during your life and have made many significant choices. You see yourself at the heart of the depressive triad of hopelessness, helplessness, and self-pity: the mental ingredients that blend with many forms of depression.

This form of helplessness is learned, and you can unlearn it. To start, look for a way to make a change—even the smallest step can help you start to shake free of your mental bonds.

The founder of Recovery Inc., psychiatrist Abraham Low (1950), points out how our language blocks change by creating an artificial sense of helplessness. He notes that people who describe their lives using *temperamental lingo*—for example, "unbearable," "intolerable," "uncontrollable"—sabotage their ability to do better. They tangle themselves in minutiae and avoid the business of change because they make themselves think change is beyond their reach. Low suggests using a *spotting technique* to tune into such language that triggers distress and problem avoidance. The more quickly you spot the triggering thought, the faster you can get down to the business of debunking these self-induced preludes to distress. The more you recognize how temperamental lingo links with your feelings of helplessness, the more likely you will find ways to redirect the flow of your thinking into positive channels— ones where you perceive yourself as having at least some control over your mental fate.

In cases of drastic, uncontrollable, and painful changes, often the healing solution is time—time to reflect, time to mend, or time to accept what previously was unacceptable. You live moment by moment, hour by hour, until the pain becomes a part of the past. During the healing time, you also can hope, pray, and rely on your religion for comfort. You can work with others for support. Finally, armed with the understanding that healing takes time, you can do much of what you normally do. Daily life continues. So, even in drastic situations where you initially can't control an outcome, you still have the potential to achieve mastery over other parts of your life.

Here is another method. Suppose you feel helpless when you deal with difficult people. You don't like this sensation but believe you can't change because difficult people have always brought on this reaction. You justify your feelings by saying, "I can't deal with this person. I'll feel pressured and overwhelmed." Now pretend that a panel of different-colored buttons appears whenever you go near a difficult person. To feel helpless you must push your helplessness button. To feel in command, you must push your "I can do something different" button. Next time you deal with a difficult person, think of those buttons. Take responsibility for choosing and then pushing a button. If you push the "I can do something different" button, you have a constructive alternative.

The *I Ching* (1961), the ancient Chinese book of change, offers us another idea for dealing with difficult people: Politeness frequently defuses the annoying actions of others. Either the colored button or the politeness method can move your thoughts from helplessness to contemplating action. The message: You are not helpless if you have choices or you can develop new skills. However, even if you can't figure out what you want to do at this moment, you still have not lost any value as a person.

When you see you have choices, you can avoid feelings of learned helplessness. Paradoxically, when you choose to accept less than perfect control, you will have more control!

The Fallback Trap

Educator, philosopher, and psychologist John Dewey wrote, "The routineer's road is a ditch out of which he cannot get, whose sides enclose him, directing his course so thoroughly that he no longer thinks of his path or destination" (1922, pp. 172–173).

Many of us fall into ruts and stay there. But what of those who climb out but keep falling back?

You may be overweight. Or be shy. Or feel tired of getting pushed around. You decide to change. You make a determined effort. You gain ground and you feel pleased with your results. Now you face the second hurdle, that of maintaining the change.

Too often the results you achieve fade unless you keep up the process that led to the change. If you don't, you drift into the fall-back pattern.

Jill's history is illustrative. She had worked for ten different companies in a six-year period. She started strongly. She was efficient, energetic, and productive. Then, after about a month, she would decide it was time to get a promotion and pay raise. She convinced herself she was better than her co-workers, so why shouldn't she advance now? Each time she took her case to her supervisors and asked for a promotion, they told her to wait. She became disgruntled and found a new entry-level job.

Jill came to me and I helped her see where her demands got her—a revolving door job pattern and feelings of futility and depression. She resolved to face the problem and stop whining about promotions and pay raises. Her second step included working effectively for 18 months before suggesting to her manager that she believed she could give more to the organization. A year later, management offered her a supervisory job and Jill took it. She is now working hard to move to the next level.

Change for the sake of change is a special fallback pattern because the change may be no change at all. For example, in late winter Felix has always done his yearly emotional housecleaning, dumping his latest woman friend, circulating his résumé, and moving to a new apartment. He does this to wipe the slate clean and to have a fresh start. Yet, all he does is whirl inside a revolving door.

Felix sees himself as a debonair master of change. Yes, he yearly changes mates, work, and location. Still, what he believes is that change is not a productive change at all.

Felix wrongly believes his problem is failing to find the right woman, the right job, or the right apartment. We could conclude from his behavior that his real problem is terror of making a commitment, but this is a wrong diagnosis. Fortunately, Felix's pattern changed when I showed him that his midwinter edginess was a symptom of a seasonal affective disorder syndrome (SADS) that had more to do with his body chemistry than his life circumstances. He discovered he could live through this without turning his life upside down. Once he labeled the problem SADS, he changed for the better by making no significant changes during this sensitive period.

Fortunately, there are many ways to break the fallback trap. One of the more effective ways is to make the effort to keep your momentum going beyond the point where you feel like quitting. You may find, then, that you have caught your second wind. Reminding yourself forcefully that you know the path you're on is beneficial can help you overcome those seductive urges to revert to old habits. Sometimes you have to allow your better judgment to prevail over equally strong avoidance wishes.

The Conflict-Avoidance Trap

If you had no yearnings or preferences or wishes, you'd have no conflicts or reasons to make changes. Thus, a conflict-free life is probably undesirable, and certainly unattainable.

You don't have to enjoy conflict, nor do you have to fear it. Those who fear conflict often follow the path of least resistance. To avoid conflict, they acquire various problem habits: procrastination, substance abuse, overeating, shortness of temper, whining and complaining, helplessness, and depression. They double their problems by feeding into feelings of inferiority that come from avoiding conflict.

Many conflicts we have with ourselves are pseudo-conflicts. They arise when our impossible dreams clash with reality. For example, you are engaging in pseudo-conflict when you:

- Act aloof and indifferent yet want to have people love and adore you

- Want to binge on food and still lose weight

- Expect to grow wise without effort

- Expect to take risks without consequence

- Expect to advance with comfort

- Indulge every whim yet want to live a rewarding life

- Insist on perfection but want to feel tolerant

When you don't solve these pseudo-problems, your tolerance for frustration drops further and you subsequently become more vulnerable to emotional distress. If you waste your time demanding what you can't have, your accomplishments will be fewer and your temper will be short. Fortunately, you can break this pattern by recognizing the absurdity of the conflict and then putting your effort into what you *can* accomplish.

Each pseudo-conflict contains an absurdity. You can't lose weight and still binge on fattening food. If you insist on perfection, you can't feel tolerant. When you want both comfort and change, you will find that the two rarely coexist.

The Complacency Trap

Complacency is the state induced by the belief that we have all the answers and have nothing more to learn. Complacency, a smug satisfaction with the status quo, makes us act like goose-stepping automatons. Complacency has two close relatives:

- *Deadly inertia,* from which ooze the sluggish habits of routine

- *Apathy,* which is the parent of inaction

Complacency, inertia, and apathy are like blind spots. When you have blind spots you will figuratively bump into the same wall again and again, and repeatedly blame the wall for your lumps. You won't see that you are the one who does the bumping.

The good news is that you can change these smothering attitudes and behavior patterns by forcing yourself to examine and test new ideas and actions. And there is an economy to this effort. When you rid yourself of the beliefs that breed complacency, you also uproot inertia and apathy.

The Limitations Trap

It's surprising how many people have real strengths that they don't recognize as strengths, or that they take for granted, or that they assume are not worthwhile because they were acquired too easily. Sometimes we even mistake a strength for a weakness.

I'd like to share several key points about the limitations trap:

- Due to a paralyzed perspective, you can confuse strengths for weaknesses and act out those misjudgments.

- We tend to hold to our illusions as though our lives depended on them. Only when an even bigger threat emerges—say, by accident—do we question them.

- The beliefs that stop us from making useful changes are rarely, if ever, external. What slows us down and frustrates us is usually something about ourselves.

- Fear often does a lot more harm than the experience we are afraid of.

- When we act out of a distorted perspective, we can't access some of our hidden strengths.

One way to overcome the trap is by turning a limitation into an asset. Although this conversion is not *always* possible, you can usually find many ways to turn a problem into an advantage. People who load their minds with trivial criticisms have a real asset when a problem requires a keen detailed critical analysis. But you can also discover assets in other ways. If you think you can't draw pictures, take lessons and practice drawing. When you think you are too dependent, you can learn independence by acting on your own! If you think that you are not effective when you speak before groups, then practice public speaking. Perhaps you have a hidden strength awaiting discovery.

POSTSCRIPT

Your decision to change involves complex mental processes, a good portion of which entails resolving a conflict between what is safe and what is challenging. When you resist challenge because of a perfectionistic fear of failure, or for any other change-blocking reason, you keep doing emotionally hurtful things to yourself. You continue the destructive behavior because it is familiar and appears safer than the change.

You start rolling the ball of change when you hear your inner voice of resistance and challenge the voice by thoughts and actions. This is the path to discovering your true assets.

16

Overcoming Procrastination

In the primordial days of human history, our ancestors foraged through the rain forests and tundra for food. Then, procrastination was not an issue. If you didn't get off your duff and scavenge for food, you went hungry. As the years passed, we discovered that we could grow and store our own food. We formed societies when we discovered that we had safety in numbers. As an ingenious species, we created traditions, laws, government, roles, symbols, and other organizing structures to regulate our conduct and commerce for the common good. We invented time and used it to regulate our lives. We brought ourselves to the point where organized and prompt responses promote financial gain, emotional growth, and physical health. At last, we also brought ourselves to a point in our evolution where individuals could put things off and still survive!

Today, procrastination is among the top impediments to change and the source of many jokes.

- Abdu, the tour guide, smiled and said, "It took one hundred years to build this pyramid."
  "Ah," said a tourist, "a government project."

- Procrastinators put off until tomorrow what they have already put off yesterday.

- The procrastinator's definition of planning is "the art of putting off today what you have no intention of doing tomorrow."

Despite the fun generated through jokes like these, this delaying pattern is no laughing matter. Chronic procrastination is a painful habit that is as difficult to overcome as quitting smoking—perhaps more so. Procrastinators deplete their personal efficiency as they squander many opportunities.

Millions defer corrective actions and tolerate repeated procrastination relapses. In this procrastinator's world, small, annoying drips accumulate and swell to floods of misery. Still, this is not a condition to feel guilt over; rather, it is a pattern to understand and change. So, in this chapter we'll look into procrastination: the causes, the varieties, and the remedies. We'll end with a follow-through plan to overcome this deadly barrier to change.

WHAT IS PROCRASTINATION?

In many instances, we have considerable latitude for getting things done. We face deadlines, of course—term papers or reports have due dates; taxes must be paid on time—yet, we have much discretion on how and when to complete our tasks. Further, it's rare that any one of us will not be late on at least some things in our life. Indeed, highly paid executives are efficient about 40 to 60 percent of the time. There are simply many unanticipated distractions as well as self-created distractions that get in the way of effective actions.

Not all procrastination is alike, and we rarely find a person who is a total procrastinator or one who never procrastinates. Procrastination is variable and exists on a sliding scale—you may poke along, then suddenly find a surge of energy to finish what you had put off. Procrastination can be definitional. The acts that constitute procrastination can vary from region to region, occupation to occupation, and country to country. Although there are overlapping features, procrastination is not the same as laziness, which is an aversion or disinclination to work. Nor is procrastination purely an act of self-indulgence.

So what is procrastination? Procrastination is needlessly putting off or delaying a relevant activity until another day or time. There are two main ways to procrastinate: (1) needlessly postponing, putting off, or delaying priority activities, and (2) substituting low-quality for high-quality efforts and results.

Needless postponement includes figuring taxes at the eleventh hour, letting dishes pile up in the sink, or showing up late for meetings. Many isolated procrastination acts, such as putting off mowing the lawn, letting a discount coupon expire, or waiting to read an overdue library book, may cause no meaningful harm. Procrastination really promotes disadvantage when people put off *quality activities* such as losing weight, facing up to tough problems, or establishing a consistent pattern of behaviors that supports their rational self-interests. During this premeditated waiting period, many feel overwhelmed, guilty, hostile, anxious, and depressed. As a byproduct, one's lateness and delays may inconvenience others. When procrastination rises to a level of high annoyance, procrastinators lose opportunities, however talented they might otherwise be!

CAUSES OF PROCRASTINATION

Procrastination is a problem habit affecting many different kinds of people. Depressed people find it tough to get started on a task. Rebellious people put off tasks to hinder others. Passive-aggressive people show up late to irritate others. Daydreamers prefer fantasy to activity. Disorganized people must concentrate to act efficiently, but they rarely do. Catch-up artists delude themselves into thinking they can only perform under pressure or when they have practically no other choice. Escapists avoid what they don't want to do. Miscast people get tangled in roles and jobs that don't fit their temperament, interests, or preferences and procrastinate on being what they could become. People who fear failure will try to avoid conditions that evoke these fears—even those experiences that clearly are on the path to constructive changes. Perfectionists often get caught up in inconsequential details and berate themselves for minor delays while neglecting the more central parts of life. Any one of us can think to do something, put too much trust in our memories, get side-tracked, then forget.

Among the various causes of procrastination, there are two — self-doubts and discomfort dodging — that link, to varying degrees, with all of the types just noted.

Self-Doubts

We all feel insecure sometimes. It is normal to feel apprehensive in new situations until we can see what is happening and get our bearing. Unfortunately, some of us repeatedly fail to act because we doubt ourselves, and thus we create our own continuing sense of insecurity.

Self-doubters are people who feel unsure of themselves and waste their time second-guessing themselves, hesitating, and worrying. Many fear the unknown because they believe they can't cope. They avoid the project to escape the tension arising from their self-doubts and then doubt themselves because they didn't complete the project.

In westernized cultures, we often link our use of time to our sense of worth because using time efficiently and effectively is a cultural value. We decide that if we use time well, we are good people. If we misuse time, we are worthless. Thus self-doubts arise when we use our time ineffectively.

There is a connection between this time–worth link and depression. The depressed look at life in this way: They feel hopeless, helpless, and (frequently) sorry for themselves. They doubt themselves. That attitude suggests why action is among the best remedies for depression — even deep and serious depressions! You show yourself (1) that what you do can make a difference, (2) that you are not helpless, and (3) that you have choices and one of those choices is that you can get things done — even when you feel depressed!

Discomfort Dodging

The founder of psychoanalysis, Sigmund Freud, called it the "id." Gestalt therapist Fritz Perls called it the "wheedler." The father of Recovery Inc., Abraham Low (1950), called it "comfort lingo."

What does the "it" in these different systems have in common? The "it" stands for strong short-sighted urges for immediate gratification and for avoiding exposure to normal discomfort.

Discomfort dodgers avoid inconveniences at all costs. Thus, they put off unpleasant tasks until not doing them becomes more inconvenient than doing them.

How do you know if you have fallen into this discomfort-dodging trap? Listen for a *delaying* voice that says, "I don't want to right now!" Listen for *awfulizing,* as in "inconvenience is horrible." Listen for the *whimpering* voice: "Poor me. I can't take the pressure." These voices carry loud discomfort-dodging messages.

Some procrastinators refuse to face their tension and go for specious rewards or a quick fix. Example: People who want to quit smoking but continue anyway may put off quitting because they fear the effects of nicotine withdrawal. As a result, they never become relaxed nonsmokers because they believe they can't bear to face the uptight stages of change that will get them there.

Abraham Low noted, "it is the anticipation of discomfort and nothing else that causes the apprehension" (p. 142). Not surprisingly, habitual reliance on shortcut solutions results in more tension, less security, higher anxiety, procrastination, and fewer long-term rewards.

PROCRASTINATION DIVERSIONS

Why don't people kick the procrastination habit if this pattern is so damaging? The answer is that we fool ourselves into thinking that "better days are coming." To make this lie more appetizing, we semiconsciously distort our perspective through emotional, action, and mental diversions. When you recognize and understand these traps, they lose much — but not all — of their power.

We also fall into the diversion trap in an ill-fated effort to safeguard unrealistic self-definitions, to avoid feeling uncomfortable, and to support the habit of avoiding inconveniences that we could promptly deal with but prefer to defer. The problem with these diversionary systems is that they complicate our lives and they eventually backfire. Let's examine the three key diversions so that you can identify them and begin to fight them.

Emotional Diversions

People caught in the emotional diversion trap wait to feel *right* before they act. Examples: Carl doesn't want to change until he feels comfortable. He believes, "I must feel secure before I act but I can't act until I feel secure." Since he rarely feels comfortable, he rarely acts. As a result, he keeps going around and around with himself and puts things off and continues to feel panicked about falling behind. Tina thinks about how depressed she feels. Then she tells herself she doesn't have the energy to get started because she is too depressed. She keeps giving herself emotional excuses, procrastinates, and feels worse. She is another victim of this low-frustration-tolerance circular thinking process.

Guilt becomes an emotional diversion when you believe you *should not* delay action and you are *worthless* because you put things off. Although procrastination costs when you let your priorities slide, condemning yourself for having a procrastination problem rarely helps spark a change. Better to get tough with the procrastination problem and change the pattern. Remember, you are *more* than a procrastinator.

Action Diversions

Action diversions involve substituting one action to avoid another. Examples: Wally wants to clean his apartment. As he looks around him, he sees dustballs on the floor, newspapers scattered about, and clutter everywhere. Instead of cleaning, he calls a friend, takes a walk, then reads the newspaper. As a result, Wally stays unhappy about his cluttered apartment. Kim has a report due. So she goes to the refrigerator and snacks. Then she watches TV. She doodles. She walks the dog. She feels the pressure build. At the last minute she hastily puts the report together. She tells herself she works better under pressure. The result is mediocre.

Action diversions come in many other forms. There is *drifting*, where the person flitters from one thing to another without visible intent and purpose other than to continue existing. The drifter mostly reacts and rarely initiates change. There are *intrigue creators* who stir up trouble to occupy themselves in the mischief they create. *Behavioral procrastinators* make great plans but rarely follow through. For them, planning is an end unto itself. *Spectators* watch what others do, then compare what they could do against these standards. They fear they won't measure up and quit before they start.

Some action diversions are like taking addictive substances. People engage in these "addictivities" whenever they feel compelled to avoid an unpleasant task. They substitute shopping, snacking, and phoning friends. Like shooting dope, addictive actions temporarily take the mind off unpleasant realities but lead to worse problems.

Mental Diversions

Some procrastinators play mental tricks on themselves. I'll discuss the four most common: the mañana trap, the contingency mañana trap, the catch 22 trap, and the backward trap.

THE MAÑANA TRAP

The mañana ploy is to wait until tomorrow to do what you could do today. People fall into this trap at any age. The seven-year-old who says, "I'll put out the garbage after I watch Donald Duck on TV," uses mañana to put off a chore he does not want to do. The teenager who says she'll do her homework after she comes back from meeting her friends at the mall uses the same mañana ploy. You hear the ring of mañana in people who say, "I'll do my taxes this weekend," and then don't. The ploy often works because we get randomly reinforced for using it. Often there are no real consequences—you throw the garbage out later. In the meantime you feel better because you made a decision even though you don't follow through. After all, there is always tomorrow.

This is a common but dangerous trap. When you are caught in the mañana trap, you go around and around as you hope that a task you find disagreeable today will become palatable tomorrow.

People caught in the mañana trap think that *later* is the opposite of *now* because later our tasks get done. They rarely do!

THE CONTINGENCY MAÑANA TRAP

People caught in the contingency mañana trap make one act contingent on another, then put off both activities. Example: "I'll lose weight when I feel motivated." Of course, how often do you feel such a sustained motivation?

Elmer wants to get into shape so he'll look good on the beach. In fantasy, he sees himself with rippling muscles, surrounded by admiring women. He tells himself he will start exercising when he finds weight-lifting equipment at the right price. He doesn't look for the equipment.

Linda believes that her priority task, to get her report finished, is a waste of time "right now." It's better to do what she feels like doing now, which is hanging out until she feels inspired. Then when she feels inspired she'll get on with the task. Sadly, the moment of inspiration does not come and the task stays undone.

THE CATCH 22 TRAP

The catch 22 ploy deserves special recognition because in this trap, there is no escape from procrastination. Here procrastinators identify fatal flaws in their appearance or character or ability that they believe permanently excuses their inaction.

Barbara wants to move into a high management position, but she tells herself she needs an M.B.A. degree to get it. She then tells herself she'll probably fail to get the degree because she is too old to pass the examinations. She does not apply for school. Result: She stays in a role that is beneath her capabilities.

Randolph wants to marry a beautiful woman with good taste. Whenever a beautiful woman thinks well of him, he assumes she has bad taste. Result: Randolph retires from life as an unhappy bachelor.

THE BACKWARD TRAP

Some well-intended people look back over their lives with regret, as we see in the parable of the thief of time.

As Drusandra walked along a woodland trail, she saw a brightly dressed dwarf rabbit running toward her. A wolverine lapped close on its trail. The woman courageously swept the little creature behind her bright blue cape and startled the wolverine, who turned tail and ran.

A relieved and grateful rabbit told her it had the power to grant her one wish for saving its life. She thought for a moment and said, "Grant me the power to relive lost moments. There were certain precious instants in my life when I lost an opportunity I now wish for. I want to experience them again."

The rabbit said, "I will grant you this wish, but beware. This gift of time is not what you might hope it will be." Drusandra insisted and the little creature gave her what she wanted.

Drusandra felt a glowing joy in her new-found power. First, she re-created the moment when she felt too frightened to allow herself to love a man she yearned for. Now that moment became a vivid reality. As she lost herself in the ecstasy of love, she wished the moment would endure. It was soon gone.

The woman recaptured many moments of what might have been. At first she felt a glow of excitement. Still, with each experience she felt regret because her present life remained the same. Indeed, as she went back to relive her precious lost moments, she found that she paid a price: She had no time to experience the present.

She could not break away from this pattern. The lost moments returned, but the experiences proved fleeting. So in despair she walked along the woodland trail to find the magical rabbit. Surely, she thought, the creature will let me live the past and the present with equal joy. That was not to be. At a turn in the trail, Drusandra saw the tattered clothing of the rabbit as it lay in testimony to the wolverine's victory.

Many people look back over their lives with regret. By magnifying the importance of lost opportunities, they trap themselves in an unsatisfying present.

Like those who paralyze themselves with sad memories, those who recall only the good times feel equally trapped. In short, focusing on the past drains energy from present efforts, and that places limits on a productive future.

TECHNIQUES FOR FOLLOW-THROUGH

The basic step to take in overcoming procrastination is to *do it now*. That's the goal. Here's how:

Start by creating a Time Goals chart to define your goals, change mechanisms, time opportunities, and results. Use four headings. Under "Desired Changes," write down no more than five changes you want to make but have put off. Under "Resources to Support Change," list the inner resources you will call upon. Under "Time Allocation," commit time to do the job. Under "Results," record the outcome.

Time is an important ingredient in this change formula. Although many people have desires and plans, few set aside the usually generous amounts of time necessary to bring about the result. When you do not make time assignments (also deadlines) and commitments, your interesting and informative ideas and plans remain incomplete. And they will remain so until you apply your time and efforts to the challenge.

If you decide to mow your lawn, you will need a defined block of time to get the job done. If you have a report to write, you will need time to draft a framework, develop supporting ideas, and draw conclusions—as well as time to rework and refine them. If you want to weigh ten pounds less, and *keep it off*, you had better plan to eat the quantity and quality of foods that will enable you to maintain that accomplishment. The time frame is the rest of your life.

Following are 15 change tactics to get you past the barrier of procrastination and start you squarely onto the path of positive change:

1. Push yourself to get routine tasks out of the way.

2. Use a simple five-minute strategy. Commit yourself to work five minutes at a priority task you have put off. After the five minutes, you decide if you will work another five minutes. If you regularly use this method, you will replace delay tactics with accomplishment.

3. Use a reverse-five-minute strategy before you start a task you normally rush. Take precisely five minutes to think and prepare before acting.

4. Take a bits-and-pieces approach: Break the task down into digestible chunks and start at the logical beginning. Block off time and sequentially tackle the problem piece by piece. Persist with this process until you achieve the results you seek. Bits and pieces does *not* mean following an isolated compartmentalized piecemeal approach where you deal with a part of the process every so often. Rather, you make a committed effort to make progress as you chip away at the challenge bit by bit.

5. Organize your project in ways that productively fit your style and personality. Assign a reasonable time to each phase. Give each phase a funny code name. Use deadlines but think of them like the time limits on "Jeopardy" or other quiz shows, rather than your final week in prison awaiting execution. Fix the deadline in your mind.

6. Complete the most pressing or important actions first.

7. Take time to think and reflect.

8. Say no to extra projects that could force you to overextend yourself.

9. Expect random and unwelcome interruptions. Deal with them directly when you can quickly get them out of the way. Otherwise, schedule them for another time.

10. Avoid the time-stickler trap where you get rigid and overprotective of your time. You'll feel too "uptight" to work effectively.

11. Allow time for casual communications that relate to your mission and goals. Use these as opportunities to add to your knowledge or to enhance your progress.

12. Allow time for productive incubation where you let your mind come up with new ideas.

13. Be sensitive to your daily rhythms. If you handle complex details more efficiently in the morning, save the afternoons for the less complex jobs.

14. Recognize that wise use of time gives you a winning edge, enhances accomplishment, and builds confidence. That is all! Avoid tying your intrinsic worth to your use of time and achievements.

15. Create a filing strategy. Set up a catch-up, keep-up, and get-ahead system. Put your initial efforts into catching up, then keeping up, and finally into stretching out to stay ahead. To use the catch-up system, place everything you have put off into the catch-up file. Then put current projects in the keep-up file. Future tasks go to the get-ahead file. The system emphasizes doing the tasks in the catch-up file to get them out of the way. Persist in getting the keep-up tasks out of the way as well. Start projects in the get-ahead file. Eventually you will put most of your energy into get-ahead efforts.

POSTSCRIPT

Procrastination is a problem habit when it becomes a persistent, nagging, frustrating pattern of postponement and delays. Since we are the architects of this plan, we also can make new plans, allot the time needed, and pace our efforts to get things done. These changes will not be accomplished by snapping our fingers or by working like tireless machines. Reversing procrastination habits takes time and practice, compromises and adjustments. It is a life-long constructive change process.

Constructive change permits no time for guilt. Banish the erroneous belief that you are a bad person because you *didn't do* what you think you *should* have done or you substituted something you think you *should not* have done. Begin to substitute responsible action for guilt, and you are on your way out of the procrastination labyrinth.

Afterword

Looking Back and Continuing the Journey

To move forward, you must do more than use the knowledge and insights gained from this book to construct an architectural plan for a new mode of living. Thinking, however profound, will not itself build your change house. Still, clear thinking can set the direction for getting the job done right. Then you figuratively pick up a hammer and pound nails into the wood to build the structure. True personal change is a process that normally begins with a solid foundation which is added to piece by piece. This is an evolutionary process. It is rarely revolutionary. It is a journey with many steps—but it doesn't begin until you take the first step.

THE HERO IN YOU

The story of the hero in everyday life illustrates some of the elements that go into your journey of change. Look at the following tale and try to see how the hero's actions are similar to what you can and might do every day.

Afterword

Pretend you are walking down a dirt road in the spring. Trees and wildflowers are a dappled mass of green foliage and white blossoms. You lose yourself for a second in the aroma of honeysuckle drifting sweetly in the air.

Suddenly your attention shifts. Moving toward you like a bevy of mindless lemmings, you see a terrified horde of people. "Head for the caves!" they shout. "It's coming." You ask what "it" might be. A man says, "The fire-spitting monster." You watch the crowd as it surges into the shallow hillside caves.

You press forward, because joining that frantic herd doesn't make sense. Who wants to hide in a cave with a panicky mob?

As you walk along the dusty road, you see more people about the roadside. Some run around confused. Others look frozen in thought. You ask why. Some of them tell you that doom looms beyond the gray horizon.

You decide to continue. As you walk farther, you see a plump, squat creature sitting in the lotus position beneath the branches of a towering willow tree. You ask, "Why are those people so panicked?"

The creature says, "They fear the dragon."

You ask, "What can I do?"

The soothsayer gazes skyward and intones, "Look for the long forked stick and the jagged white rock." You probe further, but the creature keeps chanting, "Look for the long forked stick and the jagged white rock." Miffed, you move forth, thinking that the seer is certainly mad.

For a time all remains serene. Then suddenly a shadow cloaks you in darkness. What might it be? Now you see it: A gigantic dragon with dark scaly wings, a pear-shaped torso, daggerlike claws, and smoke belching from cavernous nostrils. It moves fast. You have nowhere to run. It is too late to hide.

Fortunately, you see a long forked bough and a jagged white rock lying amid the brush at the roadside. You dive for the bough and wedge the stone into the fork. As you swing it back, the bough arches like a spring. Then you let go and hurl the stone at that scaly fire-spitting monster. Puff! The dragon disappears. The people flood from the cave and declare you a hero.

THE MEANING OF THE TALE

This tale of the everyday hero shows that people facing challenges do not worry about their self-esteem, how well they are doing, or popularity polls. Instead, they face the challenge. And it is this willingness that distinguishes heroes and heroines from those who quickly give up.

What are the other messages of this tale? One is that you can use your individual initiative and innovativeness in combination with wise counsel to overcome difficult obstacles. Timing also is important, as we saw in the hero's quick recognition of the correct application of the stone and the stick. Here are some other everyday hero guidelines:

- Feel free to ignore the false cues furnished by the crowd around you. Some people suffer from contagious helplessness and try to pass on their fears.

- It is okay to accept wise counsel; but recognize that not all counsel is wise.

- Face challenges head-on; they may not be as threatening as they first appear.

- You can assess an unknown challenge by probing it to discover what you might learn.

- You may find that mundane items in your everyday world — such as rocks and branches, whose ubiquitousness makes them easy to overlook — are useful resources.

- If you can independently pull together wise counsel, insight, and your resources, you can be an everyday hero.

The tale also carries these other basic ideas that can help you in your journey of change:

- Your intellect is a tool you can use to cope with an unpredictable world. Wisdom wins over powerful obstacles.

- You have an awareness of events that no other creature has.

Because of this intellectual awareness, you can do more than survive; you can live an abundant life!

- Thoughtful action is your way to adapt, create positive changes, and grow.

- Thought power gives you domination over claws, teeth, and bull strength!

- When you obtain useful information, you get a winning edge.

- You can rely on your inner self-regulation skills when you face periods of uncertain dangers others fear to meet.

- If you want to change, do something! You can build power when you use your creative problem-solving skills.

- Your actions have results that teach you what you can do. Feedback can be corrective. You can teach yourself what will and will not produce results.

- Each new challenge gives you an opportunity to know yourself and build yourself.

The tale implies that you are likely to learn more if you don't blindly follow the crowd. Test your ideas and look at results to shape future actions. Do this and you build competencies, master tough problems, and liberate yourself from the herd urge.

Notice that there is nothing in the story to suggest heroism is easy. Hero myths usually involve a period of lonely isolation, confrontation with self, deprivation, finding unexpected resources, conflict, and — maybe — victory. Renowned religious figures also follow this path. Jesus lived a life of sacrifice and spiritual contribution. The Buddha is said to have evolved over many lifetimes. Even the stories of our comic-book heroes and heroines contain similar elements. Batman and Supergirl live partially apart from society, face unexpected conflicts, and rely on unusual resources. They relentlessly battle the forces of evil but never quite conquer them.

Times change and so do the feats of the hero. Today you see men and women struggling to complete twenty-six-mile marathons, to build companies, or simply to communicate with each other. We also see people struggling to manage uncertain conditions, challenge themselves, and overcome destructive habits.

Most of us have the power to face and overcome fear and to use our mental and physical resources to advantage. The path we follow is that of awareness, action, assimilation (integration), acceptance, and actualization. When you regularly follow this process, you walk the path of the hero.

The everyday hero does not have to perform visible feats of physical daring. *The process counts as much as the deed.* You can attain hero status simply by squarely facing your problems and by stretching a little farther than most others.

GUIDELINES FOR CHANGE: A WRAP-UP

To light the path of the hero, I have no fixed lists of do's and don't's because there is no one best way for everyone to change. But throughout this book, I have given you some guideposts that I hope will illuminate your path of change. Let's go over them quickly. You can refer back to this list whenever you need a refresher.

- You orchestrate your experiences.

- You are responsible for how you feel and what you do.

- Your values give direction to your life.

- You can build a healthy congruity between your rational thoughts, your emotions, and your behavior.

- You choose what you do in life. If you don't like the results, you can make different choices.

- Most problem situations contain alternatives. Look for them.

- You make better progress when you think out where you want to go, define how to get there, then act.

- You must be willing to risk failure if you wish to gain mastery over your life.

- A good sense of humor helps keep matters in perspective.

- You can profit from wise counsel; you can be a sage to yourself.

- Perspective is your reality. The more realistic your perspective, the greater your chances for purposeful change.

- High frustration tolerance and self-confidence bind together to create a sense of inner security.

- You can kick practiced problem habits by developing substitute activities that supplant them.

- You can forge a satisfying career by working hard at developing your natural talents into profitable skills.

- The key to follow-through is focused, organized, persistent, and constructive efforts directed toward attaining meaningful goals. In this process it normally is preferable to also allow time for fun, games, and relaxation.

- What you believe about your ability to assert control over your inner and outer worlds is an important perspective.

- To make a significant change (or contribution), you often will do better when you schedule adequate blocks of time and focus your efforts to advance a specific interest.

- Most needless emotional misery results from either–or demands or circular thinking. You can change this through developing your perspective-building skills.

- You'll have more control over your life when you set the direction and follow through.

- Most personal change begins with an awareness and action process where you work to develop your positive attributes and conditions and diminish the effects of discretionary weaknesses.

- When you have a sense of control within, you can more ably handle the changes that happen outside of yourself.

POSTSCRIPT

Change is ubiquitous. Thus there is always something fresh to discover about change. The process is endless. But this book must end somewhere, so I'll finish it with a bit of advice: No need to wait for the muses from Mount Olympus to bring creative inspiration into your life. Start now and let the inspiration come from what you do.

Bibliography

You may find some of the following references helpful in furthering your understanding about the process of change and for developing additional ideas about applying change strategies to your own life. Thus, I have marked references with a bullet (•) to show self-help materials that you can use to help advance your change interests. For readers who are especially interested in academic or clinical issues about change, I have marked those references with an asterisk (*). Reference topics such as illusions, stress, emotions, or deception usually contain those words in the title. I have not highlighted these special-interest topics.

Adler, A. (1927). *Understanding human nature*. Garden City, N.Y.: Garden City Publishing.

Adorno, T. W., Frenkel-Brunswick, E., Levinson, D. J., & Sanford, R. N. (1950). *The authoritarian personality*. New York: Harper & Row.

Aesop's fables. (1912). New York: Avenel.

Ainslie, G. (1975). Specious reward: A behavioral theory of impulsiveness and behavior control. *Psychological Bulletin*, 82, 463–496.

Albee, G. W. (1979). The next revolution: Primary prevention of psychopathology. *Clinical Psychologist*, 32(3), 16–23.

Albee, G. W. (1986). Towards a just society. *American Psychologist*, 41(8), 891–898.

Alloy, L. B., Abrahamson, L. Y., & Viscusi, D. (1981). Induced mood and the illusion of control. *Journal of personality and social psychology*, 41, 1129–1140.

Alloy, L. B., & Clements, C. M. (1992). Illusion of control: Invulnerability to negative affect and depressive symptoms after laboratory and natural stressors. *Journal of Abnormal Psychology*, 101(2), 234–245.

Bibliography

Allport, G. W. (1937). *Pattern and growth in personality.* New York: Holt.

Arnold, M. A. (1960). *Emotion and personality* (Vol. 1). New York: Columbia University Press.

Ashford, S. J. (1988). Individual strategies for coping with stress during organizational transitions. *Journal of Applied Behavioral Science*, 24(1), 19–36.

Ayer, A. J. (1956). *The problem of knowledge.* London: Macmillan Co.

Bain, A. (1859). *The emotions and the will.* London: Longmans Green.

Bandura, A. (1982). Self-efficacy mechanism in human agency. *American Psychologist*, 37(2), 122–147.

Bandura, A. (1986). The explanatory and prescriptive scope of self-efficacy theory. *Journal of Clinical and Social Psychology*, 4, 359–373.

Bandura, A. (1990). Perceived self-efficacy in the exercise of control over AIDS infection. Special issue: Evaluation of AIDS prevention and education programs. *Evaluation & Program Planning*, 13(1), 9–17.

Barker, T., & Carter, D. (1990). Fluffing up the evidence and covering your ass: Some conceptual notes on police lying. *Deviant Behavior*, 11(1), 61–73.

Beardsley, M. (1956). *Thinking straight* (2nd ed.). Englewood Cliffs, N.J.: Prentice-Hall.

Berlyne, D. E. (1960). *Conflict, arousal, and curiosity.* Toronto: McGraw-Hill.

Bestman, T., et al. (Eds.). (1968). *The complete works of Voltaire.* Toronto: University of Toronto Press.

Birch, H. G. (1945). The relationship of previous experience to insightful problem solving. *Journal of Comparative Psychology*, 38(6), 367–383.

Birdwhistell, R. L. (1970). *Kinesics and context: Essays on body motion communications.* Philadelphia: University of Pennsylvania Press.

Bond, C. F., & Fahey, W. E. (1987). False suspicion and the misperception of deceit. *British Journal of Social Psychology*, 26(1), 41–46.

Brewin, C. R. (1989). Cognitive change processes in psychotherapy. *Psychological Review*, 96(3), 379–394.

Brown, J. D. (1991). Staying fit and staying well: Physical fitness as a moderator of life stress. *Journal of Personality and Social Psychology*, 60(4), 555–561.

Buck, R. (1984). *The communication of emotion*. New York: Gilford.

Cassaire, E. (1946). *Language and myth*. New York: Harper.

Coleman, W. E. (1984). Where the action isn't: Toward a rhetoric of illusion. *Etc.*, 41(3), 278–285.

Combs, A. W., and Snygg, D. (1959). *Individual behavior: A perceptual approach to behavior.* New York: Harper & Row.

*Curtis, R. C., & Stricker, G. (1991). *How people change: Inside and outside therapy*. New York: Plenum.

Darwin, C. (1872). *Emotional expressions in man and animal.* London: John Murray.

Defoe, D. (1975). *Robinson Crusoe*. M. Shinagel (Ed.), Critical Editions series. New York: Norton.

DePaulo, B. M., Kirkendol, S. E., Tang, J., & O'Brien, T. P. (1988). The motivational impairment effect in the communication of deception: Replications and extensions. Special issue: Deception. *Journal of Nonverbal Behavior*, 12(3, Pt. 1), 177–202.

DePaulo, P. J., & DePaulo, B. M. (1989). Can deception by salespersons and customers be detected through nonverbal behavioral cues? *Journal of Applied Social Psychology*, 19(18, Pt. 2), 1552–1577.

Descartes, R. (1984). Principles of philosophy. In J. Cottingham, R. Stoothoff, & D. Murdoch (Eds.), *The philosophical writings of Descartes*. Cambridge, Eng.: Cambridge University Press.

DeTurck, M. A., & Miller, G. R. (1990). Training observers to detect deception: Effects of self-monitoring and rehearsal. *Human Communication Research*, 16(4), 603–620.

Dewey, J. (1909). *Moral principles in education*. New York: Houghton Mifflin Co.

Dewey, J. (1922). *Human nature and conduct.* New York: Henry Holt and Company.

Dewey, J. (1926). *Experience and nature*. Chicago: Open Court.

•Dewey, J. (1933). *How we think*. Boston: D. C. Heath & Co.

Bibliography

Dewey J. (1960). *Theory of the moral life.* New York: Holt, Rinehart and Winston.

Dickson-Parnell, B. E., & Zeichner, A. (1985). Effects of a short-term exercise program on caloric consumption. *Health Psychology, 4*(5), 437–448.

*DiClemente, C. C., & Prochaska, J. O. (1982). Self-change and therapy change of smoking behavior: A comparison of processes of change in cessation and maintenance. *Addictive Behaviors, 7*(2), 133–142.

Doan, B. D., & Gray, R. E. (1992). The heroic cancer patient: A critical analysis of the relationship between illusion and mental health. *Canadian Journal of Behavioural Science.* Special issue: The psychology of control, 24(2), 253–266.

Drucker, P. F. (1966). *The effective executive.* New York: Harper & Row.

Dunlap, K. (1972). *Habits: Their making and unmaking.* New York: Liveright.

Durand, W. (1926). *The story of philosophy.* New York: Simon & Schuster.

Ehrlich, H. (1973). *The social psychology of prejudice.* New York: John Wiley.

Einhorn, H. J., & Holgarth, R. M. (1978). Confidence in judgment: Persistence of the illusion of validity. *Psychological Review,* 85, 395–416.

Ekman, P. (1985). *Telling lies.* New York: Norton.

Ekman, P. (1988). Lying and nonverbal behavior: Theoretical issues and new findings. Special issue: Deception. *Journal of Nonverbal Behavior,* 12(3, Pt. 1), 163–175.

Ellis, A. (1962). *Reason and emotion in psychotherapy.* Secaucus, N.J.: Lyle Stuart.

•Ellis, A. (1977). *How to live with and without anger.* New York: Readers' Digest.

•Ellis, A. (1988). *How to stubbornly refuse to make yourself miserable about anything — yes, anything.* Secaucus, N.J.: Lyle Stuart.

Ellis A. (1990). Is rational emotive therapy (RET) rationalist or constructive? In A. Ellis & W. Dryden (Eds.), *The essential Albert Ellis: Seminal writings on psychotherapy* (pp. 114–141). New York: Springer.

Ellis, A. (1991a). The philosophical basis of rational emotive therapy (RET). *Psychotherapy in Private Practice,* 8(4), 97–106.

Ellis, A. (1991b). Suggestibility, irrational beliefs, and emotional disturbance. In J. F. Schumaker (Ed.), *Human suggestibility* (pp. 309–325). New York: Routledge.

•Ellis, A., & Knaus, W. J. (1979). *Overcoming procrastination*. New York: New American Library.

Ellis, B. (1979). *Rational belief systems*. Totowa, N.J.: Rowman & Littlefield.

Engle, M. J. (1976). *With good reason: An introduction to unfound fallacies*. New York: St. Martin's Press.

Epstein, E. J. (1989). *Deception*. New York: Simon & Schuster.

Ewing, D. (1983, January–February). How to negotiate with employee objectors. *Harvard Business Review*, 103–110.

Fischoff, B. (1991). Value elicitation: Is there anything in there? *American Psychologist*, 46(8), 835–847.

Flesch, R. (1951). *The art of clear thinking*. New York: Harper Bros.

Fowler, H. (1965). *Curiosity and exploratory behavior*. New York: Macmillan.

Fox, N. A. (1991). If it's not left, it's right: Electroencephalograph asymmetry and the development of emotion. *American Psychologist*, 46(8), 863–872.

•Franklin, B. (1956). *Autobiography*. New York: Harper & Bros.

Fried, C. (1970). *An anatomy of values*. Cambridge, Mass.: Harvard University Press.

Frudengerger, H., & Richelson, G. (1980). *Burnout: The high cost of achievement*. Garden City, N.Y.: Doubleday & Co.

Fuhriman, A., Barlow, S. H., & Wanlass, J. (1989). Words, imagination, meaning: Toward change. *Psychotherapy*, 26(2), 149–156.

Gecas, V. (1989). The social psychology of self-efficacy. *Annual Review of Sociology*, 15, 291–316.

°Geller, E. (1965). *Thought and change*. Chicago: University of Chicago Press.

Gilbert, D. T. (1991). How mental systems believe. *American Psychologist*, 46(2), 107–119.

Glass, D. C. (1968). Theories of consistency and the study of personality.

Bibliography

In E. F. Borgatta & W. W. Lambert (Eds.), *Handbook of personality theory and research* (pp. 788–854). Chicago: Rand McNally.

*Goldfried M. R., & Davison, G. C. (1976). *Clinical behavior therapy*. New York: Holt, Rinehart and Winston.

Gombrich, E. H. (1956). *Art and illusion*. Princeton, N.J.: Bollingen Series.

Gotshalk, D. W. (1963). *Patterns of good and evil*. Urbana: University of Illinois Press.

Graham, A. G. (1961). *The problem of value*. London: Hutchenson University Library.

Green, L. (1978). Temporal and stimulus factors in self-monitoring by obese persons. *Behavior Therapy* 9(3), 328–341.

Hall, N. R. S., & Goldstein, A. (1986). Thinking well: The chemical links between emotions and health. *The Sciences* (New York Academy of Science), 34–41.

Hamburg, D. A., Elliott, G. R., & Parron, D. L. (Eds.). (1982). *Health and behavior frontiers of research in the biobehavioral sciences*. Washington, D.C.: National Academy Press.

Hamilton, V. (1983). *The cognitive structures and processes of human motivation and personality*. New York: John Wiley.

Handy, C. (1989). *The age of unreason*. Boston: Harvard Business School Press.

Hartman, R. (1967). *The structure of value*. Carbondale: Southern Illinois Press.

Hartnack, J. (1965). *Wittgenstein*. New York: New York University Press.

Hawton, H. (1956). *An adventure in ideas*. Greenwich, Conn.: Fawcett.

High, D. M. (1967). *Language persons and belief*. New York: Oxford Press.

Hillard, A. H. (1950). *The forms of value*. New York: Columbia University Press.

Hiram, S. (1895). *Studies in the evolutionary psychology of feelings*. New York: Macmillan & Co.

Hobfoll, S. E., Speilberger, C. D., Breznitz, S., Figley, C., Folkman, S., Lepper-Green, B., Meichenbaum, D., Milgrim, N. A., Sandler, I., Sarason I., & van der Kolk, B. (1991). War-related stress: Addressing the stress of war and other traumatic events. *American Psychologist*, 46(8), 848–855.

Hobhouse, L. T. (1921). *The rational good*. New York: Holt.

Hoffer, E. (1951). *The true believer: Thoughts on the nature of mass movements*. New York: Harper.

•Hoffer, E. (1952). *The ordeal of change*. New York: Harper & Row.

Hogan, R. (1973). Moral conduct and moral character: A psychological perspective. *Psychological Bulletin*, 79(4), 217–232.

Holmes, T. H., & Rale, R. H. (1967). The social readjustive rating scale. *Journal of Psychosomatic Research*, 11, 213–218.

*Horney, K. (1950). *Neurosis and human growth*. New York: Norton.

Humphrey, J. H. (Ed.). (1986). *Human stress: Current selected research* (Vol. 1). New York: AMS Press.

•*I Ching*. (1961). (Trans. R. Wilheim) (2nd ed.). Bolinger series XIX. Princeton, N.J.: Princeton University Press.

Izard, C. E. (1971). *The face of emotion*. New York: Appleton-Century-Crofts.

Jacobs, S. (1989). Karl Popper and Albert Ellis: Their ideas on psychology and rationality compared. *Journal of Rational-Emotive & Cognitive Behavior Therapy*, 7(3), 173–185.

•Jacobson, E. (1934). *You must relax*. New York: Whittlesey.

Jaervi, T. (1989). Synergistic effect on mortality in Atlantic salmon, salmon salar, smolt caused by osmotic stress and presence of predators. *Environment Biology Fish*, 26(2), 149–152.

James, W. (1892). *Psychology*. New York: Henry Holt.

Jastrow, J. (1928). *Keeping mentally fit*. Garden City, N.Y.: Garden City Publishing.

Jung, C. (1961). In *I Ching* (trans. R. Wilheim) (2nd ed.). Bolinger series XIX. Princeton, N.J.: Princeton University Press.

Jung, C. (1971). *Psychological types*. Princeton, N.J.: Princeton University Press.

Kagan, J., & Snidman, N. (1991). Temperamental factors in human development. *American Psychologist*, 46(8), 856–862.

Bibliography

Katz, R. C., & Singh, N. N. (1986). Reflections on the ex-smoker: Some findings on successful quitters. *Journal of Behavioral Medicine*, 9(2), 191–202.

*Kazdin, A. E. (1974). Self monitoring and behavior change. In M. J. Mahoney & C. E. Thoresen (Eds.), *Self control: Power to the person* (pp. 218–246). Monterey, Calif.: Brooks-Cole.

*Kelly, G. (1955). *The psychology of personal constructs*. New York: Norton.

Key, W. B. (1973). *Subliminal seduction*. New York: New American Library.

Keyes, R. (1982). *Chancing it: Why we take risks*. Boston: Little Brown & Co.

Kiecolt-Glaser, J. K., & Glaser, R. (1988). Major life changes, chronic stress, and immunity. In T. P. Bridge, F. K. Mirsky, & F. K. Goodwin (Eds.), *Psychological, neuropsychiatric, and substance abuse aspects of AIDS* (pp. 217–224). New York: Raven.

Kiecolt-Glaser, J. K., Kennedy, S., Kalkoff, S., Fisher, L., Speicher, C. E., & Glaser, R. (1988). Marital discord and immunity in males. *Psychosomatic Medicine*, 50, 213–229.

Kirschenbaum, D. S. (1987). Self-regulatory failure: A review with clinical implications. *Clinical Psychology Review*, 7(1), 77–104.

Kleinke, C. (1978). *Self-perception*. San Francisco: W. H. Freeman Co.

Knaus, W. J. (1973). Overcoming procrastination. *Rational Living*, 8(2), 2–7.

Knaus, W. J. (1974). *Rational emotive education: A manual for elementary school teachers*. New York: Institute for Rational Emotive Psychotherapy.

Knaus, W. J. (1975). Therapeutic techniques: Cognitive-behavior strategies for the therapeutic armentarium. *Rational Living*, 10(1), 41–43.

•Knaus, W. J. (1979). *Do it now: How to stop procrastinating*. Englewood Cliffs, N.J.: Prentice-Hall.

•Knaus, W. J. (1982a). *How to get out of a rut*. Englewood Cliffs, N.J.: Prentice-Hall.

Knaus, W. J. (1982b). The parameters of procrastination. In R. Greiger & I. Greiger (Eds.), *Cognition and emotional disturbance* (pp. 174–196). New York: Human Sciences Press.

Knaus, W. J. (1983a). Children and low frustration tolerance. In A. Ellis & M. Bernard (Eds.), *Rational-emotive approaches to the problems of childhood* (pp. 139–158). New York: Plenum.

•Knaus, W. J. (1983b). *How to conquer your frustrations*. Englewood Cliffs, N.J.: Prentice-Hall.

Knaus, W. J. (1983c). Why people procrastinate — Is there a cure? Interviewer unknown. *U.S. News & World Report*, 95(7), 61–67.

Knaus, W. J. (1985). Student burnout: A rational emotive education treatment approach. In A. Ellis & M. Bernard (Eds.), *Clinical applications of rational-emotive therapy* (pp. 257–276). New York: Plenum.

Knaus, W. J. (1988a). Deception. *Bottom Line Personal*. New York: Boardroom Reports, 9(5), 1–2.

Knaus, W. J. (1988b). Follow-through. Interview through Barry Lenson. *Executive Strategies*. New York: National Institute of Business Managers, 3(8), 1–2.

Knaus, W. J. (1990a). Are you guilty of any of these five productivity killers? Interview through Robert Hard. *Customer Services Managers' Newsletter*, 2(9), 3.

Knaus, W. J. (1990, July). Clinical change strategies: The inner world of change. Paper presented at the 1990 American Association of Mental Health Counselors convention, Keystone, Colo.

Knaus, W. J. (1990b). Problem solving. Interview through Barry Lenson. *Executive Strategies*. New York: National Institute of Business Management, 5(13), 6.

Knaus, W. J. (1991). Competence puts you ahead of your rivals. *Executive Strategies*, 6(6), 2–3.

Knaus, W. J. (1992, June). Pathological administrative practices: What they are and what to do about them. Paper presented at the 1992 World Conference of Cognitive Therapy, Toronto.

Knaus, W. J. (1992). A rational perspective on organizational change. *Journal of Cognitive Psychotherapy: An International Quarterly*, 6(4), 277–295.

•Knaus, W. J. (1993). *Rational recovery: A quick start introduction*. Longmeadow, Mass.: Wm. Knaus Associates.

•Knaus, W. J., & Hendricks, C. (1986). *The illusion trap*. New York: World Almanac.

Bibliography

Knaus, W. J., & Knaus, N. B. (1993). A rational emotive education program to help disruptive mentally retarded clients develop self-control. In W. Dryden & P. Hill (Eds.), *Innovations in rational emotive therapy* (pp. 201–217). London: Sage.

Knaus, W. J., & Wessler, R. (1975). Rational-emotive problem simulation. *Rational Living*, 11(2), 8–11.

Kockelmans, J. J., & Husserlis, E. (1967). *Phenomenological psychology*. Pittsburgh: Duquesne University Press.

Kohler, W. (1925). *The mentality of apes*. (Trans. E. Winter). New York: Harcourt, Brace & World.

Kohler, W. (1938). *The place of values in a world of facts*. New York: Liveright.

Koop, E. (1986). The health consequences of nonvoluntary smoking. Washington, D.C.: U.S. Government Printing Office.

Krotkiewski, M., Grimby, G., Holm, G., & Szczepanik, J. (1990). Increased muscle dynamic endurance associated with weight reduction on a very-low-calorie diet. *American Journal of Clinical Nutrition*, 51(3), 321–330.

Langer, E. J. (1975). The illusion of control. *Journal of Personality and Social Psychology*, 32, 311–328.

*Lazarus, A. A. (1971). *Behavior therapy and beyond*. New York: McGraw-Hill.

Lazarus, A. A. (1976). *Multimodal behavior therapy*. New York: Springer.

*Lazarus, A. A. (1989). *The practice of multimodal therapy*. Baltimore: Johns Hopkins University Press.

Lazarus, R. S. (1991). Progress on a cognitive-motivational-relational theory of emotion. *American Psychologist*, 46(8), 819–834.

Lazarus, R. S., & Cohen, J. B. (1977). Environmental stress. In I. Altman & J. F. Wohlwill (Eds.), *Human behavior and environment* (Vol. 2). New York: Plenum.

LeDoux, J. E., & Hirst, W. (Eds.). (1986). *Mind and brain: Dialogues in cognitive neuroscience*. New York: Cambridge University Press.

Lee, D. E. (1987). The self-deception of the self-destructive. *Perceptual & Motor Skills*, 65(3), 975–989.

Levenson, R. W., & Gottman, J. M. (1988). Physiological and affective predictors of change in relationship satisfaction. *Journal of Personality and Social Psychology*, 49, 85–94.

Lewin, R. (1987). Do animals read minds, tell lies? (Apparent deception widespread among monkeys & apes). *Science*, 238, 1350–1352.

Lindskold, S., & Han, G. (1986). Intent and the judgment of lies. *Journal of Social Psychology*, 126(1), 129–130.

Lippard, P. V. (1988). Ask me no questions, I'll tell you no lies: Situational exigencies for interpersonal deception. *Western Journal of Speech Communication*, 52(1), 91–103.

Littlepage, G. E., Tang, D. W., & Pineault, M. A. (1986). Nonverbal and content factors in the detection of deception in planned and spontaneous communications. *Journal of Social Behavior & Personality*, 1(3), 439–450.

Loftus, E. E. (1993). The reality of repressed memories. *American Psychologist*, 48(5), 518–537.

•Low, A. (1950). *Mental health through will training*. Boston: Christopher Publishing House.

•Mahoney, M. (1979). *Self-change: Strategies for solving personal problems*. New York: Norton.

*Mahoney, M. (1991). *Human change processes*. New York: Basic Books.

*Mann, J. (1965). *Changing human behavior*. New York: Charles Scribner.

Marlatt, G. A., & George, W. H. (1984). Relapse prevention: Introduction and overview of the model. *British Journal of Addiction*, 79(3), 261–273.

•May, R. (1975). *The courage to create*. New York: Norton.

McCarran, M. S., & Andrasik, F. (1990). Behavioral weight-loss for multiply-handicapped adults: Assessing caretaker involvement and measures of behavior change. *Addictive Behaviors*, 15(1), 13–20.

McCormack, S. A., & Levine, T. R. (1990). When lies are uncovered: Emotional and relational outcomes of discovered deception. *Communication Monographs*, 57(2), 119–138.

McDougal, W. (1926). *An introduction to social psychology*. Boston: John W. Luce.

McGill, J. V. (1954). *Emotions and reason*. Springfield, Ill.: Charles Thomas.

Bibliography

*Meichenbaum, D. (1977). *Cognitive-behavior modification: An integrative approach*. New York: Plenum.

Meichenbaum, D., & Jaremko, M. (1983). *Stress reduction and prevention*. New York: Plenum.

Mendler, A. E. (1947). *Logic for the millions*. New York: Philosophical Library.

Morris, C. (1956). *Varieties of human value*. Chicago: University of Chicago Press.

Murphy, G. (1958). *Human potentials*. New York: Basic Books.

Nietzsche, F. W. (1958). *Thus spoke Zarathustra*. (Trans. A. Tille). London: Dent.

Nietzsche, F. W. (1967). *The will to power*. New York: Random House.

Odio, M., Goliszek, A., Brodish, A., & Ricardo, M. J. (1986). Impairment of immune function after cessation of long-term chronic stress. *Immunological Letter*, 13(1–2), 25–31.

O'Hair, D., Cody, M. J., & Behnke, R. R. (1985). Communication apprehension and vocal stress as indices of deception. *Western Journal of Speech Communication*, 49(4), 286–300.

Owen, N., Halford, W., Kim, U. & Adelaide, S. A. (1988). Psychology, public health, and cigarette smoking. *Australian Psychologist*, 23(2), 137–152.

Palmieri, L. E. (1960). *Language and clear thinking*. Lincoln, Neb.: Johnsen.

•Payot, J. (1893). *The education of the will*. New York: Funk & Wagnalls Co.

Pearson, C. S. (1989). *The hero within*. New York: Harper & Row.

•Peck, S. M. (1978). *The road less traveled*. New York: Simon & Schuster.

Pennebaker, J. W. (1991). *Opening up: The healing power of confiding in others*. New York: Avon.

Perls, F. S. (1969). *Gestalt therapy verbatim*. Lafayette, Calif.: Real People Press.

Perls, F. S., Hefferline, R. F., & Goodman, P. (1951). *Gestalt therapy*. New York: Dell.

Perry, R. B. (1926). *General theory of values*. Cambridge, Mass.: Harvard University Press.

Peterson, C., & Bossio, L. M. (1991). *Health and optimism*. New York: Free Press.

Piaget, J., & Inhelder, B. (1975). *The origin of ideas and choice in children*. New York: Norton.

Piani, A. L., & Schoenborn, C. A. (1993). *Health promotion and disease prevention: United States, 1990*. Washington, D.C. Health and Human Services Dept., Public Health Service, Centers for Disease Control and Prevention, National Center for Health Statistics, Division of Health Interview Statistics.

Pickering, A. D. (1989). Environmental stress and the survival of brown trout and Salmo trutta. *Freshwater Biology*, 21(1), 47–56.

Pickering, A. D., & Pottinger, T. G. (1988). Lymphocytopenia and the overwinter survival of Atlantic salmon parr and Salmo salar. *Journal of Fish Biology*, 32(5), 689–697.

Plato, Epictetus, & Marcus Aurelius. (1909). The Harvard Classics. New York: P. F. Collier.

Pope, W. R., & Forsyth, D. R. (1986). Judgments of deceptive communications: A multidimensional analysis. *Bulletin of the Psychonomic Society*, 24(6), 435–436.

Popper, K. R. (1965). *Conjecture and reflections: The growth of scientific knowledge*. New York: Basic Books.

Popper, K. R. (1983). *Realism and the aim of science*. Totowa, N.J.: Rowman & Littlefield.

*Prochaska, J. O., DiClemente, C. C., & Norcross, J. C. (1992). In search of how people change: Applications to addictive behavior. *American Psychologist*, 47(9), 1102–1114.

Purington, J. R., & Clifford, M. (1983). *Management's role for reducing employee stress* (final report). Leadership and Management Development Center, Maxwell AFB, Ala. Report No. LMDC-TR-83–1, 1–38.

Purtill, R. L. (1972). *Logical thinking*. New York: Harper & Row.

Rakowski, W., Wells, B. L., Lasater, T. M., & Carleton, R. A. (1991). Correlates of expected success at health habit change and its role as a predictor in health behavior research. *American Journal of Preventive Medicine*, 7(2), 89–94.

Bibliography

Rale, R. H. (1978). The pathway between subjects' recent life changes and their near future illness reports. In R. B. Dohenwerd & B. Dohenwerd (Eds.), *Stressful life events: Their nature and effects*. New York: John Wiley.

Rappaport, D. (1959). *Emotions and memory*. New York: International Universities Press.

Rath, L., Harmin, M., & Simon, S. (1966). *Values and teaching*. Columbus, Ohio: Charles Merrill.

Reisenzein, R., & Schönpflug, W. (1992). Stumpf's cognitive-evaluative theory of emotion. *American Psychologist, 47*(1), 34–45.

Renne, K. S. (1971). Health and marital experience in an urban population. *Journal of marriage and the family, 23*, 3338–3350.

Robinson, D. N. (1993). Is there a Jamesian tradition in psychology? *The American Psychologist, 48*(6), 638–643.

Rogers, C. R. (1951). *Client-centered therapy: Its current practice, implications and theory*. Boston: Houghton Mifflin.

Rogers, C. R. (1969). *Freedom to learn*. Columbus, Ohio: Charles Merrill.

Rokeach, M. (1971). Long range experimental modification of values, attitude, and behavior. *American Psychologist, 26*, 453–459.

Rokeach, M. (1973). *The nature of human values*. New York: The Free Press.

Rosenwald, G. C. (1985). Hypocrisy, self-deception, and perplexity: The subject's enhancement as methodological criterion. *Journal of Personality & Social Psychology, 49*(3), 682–703.

Ruchlis, H. (1962). *Clear thinking*. New York: Harper & Row.

Russell, B. (1958). *The will to doubt*. New York: Philosophical Press.

Ryle, G. (1954). *Dilemmas*. Cambridge, Eng.: Cambridge University Press.

Sartre, J. P. (1948). *The emotions: Outline of a theory*. New York: Philosophical Press.

Schactner, S. (1964). The introduction of cognitive and physiological determinants of emotional states. In L. Berkowitz (Ed.), *Advances in experimental social psychology* (Vol. 7). New York: Academic Press.

Schactner, S., & Singer, J. T. (1962). Cognitive, social, and physiological determinants of emotional states. *Psychological Review*, 69, 379–399.

Seligman, M. E. P. (1975). *Helplessness: On depression, development and death.* San Francisco: W. H. Freeman.

Selye, H. (1956). *The stress of life.* New York: McGraw-Hill.

Selye, H. (1980). *Selye's guide to stress reduction.* New York: Van Nostrand Reinhold Co.

Sherif, C., Sherif, M., & Nebergall, R. E. (1965). *Attitude and attitude change.* Philadelphia: W. B. Saunders.

Sherin, H. (1915). *Individual mastery: How to make the most of yourself.* New York: The Trow Press.

Sitton, S. C., & Griffin, S. T. (1981). Detection of deception from clients' eye contact patterns. *Journal of Counseling Psychology*, 28(3), 269–271.

Slovic, P., Fischoff, B., & Liechtenstein, S. (1981). Perception and acceptability of risk from energy systems. In A. Baum & J. E. Singer (Eds.), *Advances in environmental psychology* (Vol. 3, pp. 155–170). Hillsdale, N.J.: Erlbaum.

Snyder, C. R. (1989). Reality negotiation: From excuses to hope and beyond. Special issue: Self-illusions: When are they adaptive? *Journal of Social & Clinical Psychology*, 8(2), 130–157.

Somers, A. R. (1979). Marital status, health, and use of health services. *Journal of the American Medical Association*, 241, 1818–1822.

Sperry, R. W. (1991, August). Impact and promise of the cognitive revolution. Paper presented at the 99th Annual American Psychological Association Convention, San Francisco.

Stewart, C. (1956). *Guides to straight thinking: With 13 common fallacies.* New York: Harper & Bros.

Stoudemire, A., Frank, R., Hedemark, N., Kamlet, M., & Blazer, D. (1986). The economic burden of depression. *General hospital psychiatry*, 8(6), 387–394.

Strichartz, A. F., & Burton, R. V. (1990). Lies and truth: A study of the development of the concept. *Child Development*, 61(1), 211–220.

Sully, J. (1884, May). Illusions: A psychological study. *Humbolt Library*, 56, 339–440.

Bibliography

Szent-Györgyi, A. (1963). *Science ethics and politics*. New York: Vantage Press.

Taylor, S. E., Collins, R. L., Skokan, L. A., & Aspinwall, L. G. (1989). Maintaining positive illusions in the face of negative information: Getting the facts without letting them get to you. Special issue: Self-illusions: When are they adaptive? *Journal of Social & Clinical Psychology*, 8(2), 114–129.

Thouless, R. H. (1939). *How to think straight*. New York: Simon & Schuster.

Titchner, E. B. (1908). *Lectures on the elementary psychology of feelings and attitude*. New York: Macmillan.

Toffer, A. (1972). *The futurists*. New York: Random House.

*Toynbee, A. J. (1966). *Change and habit*. New York: Oxford University Press.

•Trimpey, J. (1992). *The small book* (rev. ed.). New York: Delacorte.

Vialettes, B., Ozanon, J. P., Kaplansky, S., Farnarier, C., Sauvaget, E., Lassmann-Vague, V., Bernard, D., & Vague, P. (1989). Stress antecedents and immune status in recently diagnosed type I (insulin dependent) diabetes mellitus. *Diabetic Metabolism*, 15(1), 45–50.

Wagenaar, W. A., & Keren, G. B. (1988). Chance and luck are not the same. *Journal of Behavioral Decision Making*, 1(2), 65–75.

Watson, G. (1971). Resistance to change. *American Behavioral Scientist*, 14(5), 745–766.

Werkmeister, W. H. (1967). *Man and his values*. Lincoln, Neb.: University of Nebraska Press.

Whitman, W. (1961). In Gay W. Allen & E. Scully Bradley (Eds.), *Collected writings of Walt Whitman*. New York: New York University Press.

Williams, R. (1968). Values. In E. Sills (Ed.), *International encyclopedia of the social sciences*. New York: Macmillan.

•Williams, T. (1923). *Dread and besetting fears*. New York: Little John.

*Wolpe, J. (1969). *The practice of behavior therapy*. New York: Pergamon.

Wolpe, J. (1984). Deconditioning and ad hoc uses of relaxation: An overview. *Journal of Behavior Therapy & Experimental Psychiatry*, 15(4), 299–304.

Zane, N. W. (1989). Change mechanisms in placebo procedures: Effects of suggestion, social demand, and contingent success on improvement in treatment. *Journal of Counseling Psychology*, 36(2), 234–243.

*Zimbardo, P., Ebbesen, E., & Maslach, C. (1977). *Influencing attitudes and changing behavior*. Reading, Mass.: Addison-Wesley.

Zinkhan, G. M., Hong, J. W., & Lawson, R. (1990). Achievement and affiliation motivation: Changing patterns in social values as represented in American advertising. Special issue: Social values. *Journal of Business Research*, 20(2), 135–143.

Index

Index

Index

Index